ENERGY

A CURRICULUM UNIT FOR THREE, FOUR, AND FIVE YEAR OLDS

By
Carolyn S. Diener
Carmen R. Jettinghoff
Elizabeth B. Robertson
Martha P. Strickland

Cover design by Burl Compton

HUMANICS LIMITED
P.O. Box 7447
Atlanta, Georgia 30309

Copyright © 1981 by Humanics Limited. All rights reserved. No part of this book may be reproduced by any means, nor transmitted, nor translated into a machine language, without written permission from Humanics Limited.
Library of Congress Card Catalog Number: 81-83050
PRINTED IN THE UNITED STATES OF AMERICA
ISBN 0-89334-069-3

We recognize the contributions of Mrs. Anna Marie Turner, Mr. Jim Woodley, Dr. Tommie Jean Hamner, Dr. Barbara Barker and Dr. Betty Carlton.

TABLE OF CONTENTS

INTRODUCTION 1

GUIDE TO USING THE CURRICULUM 2

THE CURRICULUM

    I. ENERGY AWARENESS 5

    II. SOURCES OF ENERGY 19

    III. USES OF ENERGY 49

    IV. WISE ENERGY USE 65

APPENDICES 75

INTRODUCTION

This energy unit is designed primarily to be used with three, four and five year old children. Many of the activities are also appropriate for six and seven year olds. This unit is the outgrowth of an energy research project that was conducted at the Child Development Center, The University of Alabama. The overall objectives of the unit are to help children become aware of what energy is, the sources of energy, the uses of energy and ways to use energy wisely.

We chose to exclude any information on speculative development of new and alternative energy sources for two reasons. First, children need to acquire a foundation of the basic information which is the focus of this book. Second, the young children for whom this curriculum was developed have yet to reach the maturation level for abstract learning. Geothermal energy, synthetic fuel and other possible alternatives are still being researched. Extensive use of nuclear energy is uncertain. Concepts related to these energy possibilities are far too complex and abstract in nature for young children to comprehend.

The developmental psychologist, Erik Erikson, indicates that the developmental task of early childhood is to develop initiative—the drive to actively seek out experiences, to explore, to investigate, to do, to make and to create. During early childhood, children are rooted in the sensory world and need concrete experiences. Play is the resource by which young children experience and make sense of the external world. Children learn through play. It is a well known fact that during play experiences much of what children learn occurs by imitating adult behavior. A play environment that includes opportunities for dramatic, free and organized play allows children a chance to explore, to discover and to learn when developmentally ready.

This curriculum is based on these principles. Thus, the activities that are included in this unit are designed to help young children learn through the means by which we understand children learn best: through firsthand experiences, by manipulating materials, by discussing what is happening as it takes place, by modeling the examples set by adults, and through play.

There is increasing urgency that we all understand the realities of the worldwide energy situation and learn to use energy wisely. It is the authors' conviction that it is important for children to learn concepts relating to energy at an early age. We hope that the concepts and activities developed in this curriculum will be a first step in the understanding of energy by our children, the decision makers of tomorrow.

HOW TO USE THIS CURRICULUM

This unit is organized into the following general concepts:

> Energy Awareness
>
> Sources of Energy
>
> Uses of Energy
>
> Wise Energy Use

Each concept has been divided into more specific subconcepts. The authors have developed a wide selection of activities designed to provide children with firsthand experiences to teach each concept. Activities which help the children understand their own body energy are used as a foundation for teaching each concept, which will help make this unit more meaningful to the child.

Since the subject of energy is broad and complicated, it is important that the teacher become familiar with the topic through background reading. Appendix A contains a list of suggested reading materials for the teacher. Once the teacher is knowledgeable in the area, his or her activity selection and unit planning should be more effective.

The unit contains activities oriented toward language, science, math, art, movement and dramatic play. Some of the activities are specifically designed for the outdoors, while others can be adapted for outdoor use. The patterns for flannel-board story characters and lotto games as well as other illustrations accompany many of the activities. Appendix B provides a complete list of the books, recordings and filmstrips to be used in activities described in the unit, plus additional resources the teacher may wish to use and incorporate into the classroom activities.

Musical experiences are included as an integral part of the unit. The reader will no doubt be familiar with many songs which will be appropriate for use with this unit. Several songs are reprinted in the text, and the reader may choose additional songs from the sources listed in Appendix B.

We recommend that when using this unit the teacher choose activities which are appropriate to the developmental level and background of experiences of a particular group of children. It is advisable that the teacher select no more than three or four activities to teach each concept. The activities chosen should represent different curriculum areas (i.e., math, language, art, outdoor play, etc.) to provide the children with repeated exposure to the same concept through varied experiences.

Activities should be presented in such a way that experiences build on one another in a sequential manner. The activities relating to the same concept should be carried out on different days to allow the information presented to be absorbed by the children. We suggest that when the teacher uses the unit as a whole, he or she integrate it into the ongoing curriculum over a long period of time to keep the children's interest level high.

The teacher should develop a file of pictures from magazines and other sources relating to each of the concepts developed in this unit. These pictures may then be used for picture discussions at group times, for various games (Energy Ant, matching games, etc.) and for bulletin board displays. Bulletin boards are an effective way to stimulate discussion and interest in the children and reinforce concepts.

Parents can also help the children learn and understand the energy concepts. Informing the parents through newsletters and bulletin boards of the activities going on at school and suggesting ways they can teach some of the same concepts at home help to reinforce the universality of the information presented. Some of the ways parents may reinforce concepts at home are:

* Encouraging children to turn off lights and T.V.
* Having them participate in preparing meals
* Commenting on the way the food will give their bodies energy
* Commenting on the type of energy used to cook the food
* Turning down the thermostat and wearing more clothing

Inviting parents to come to school and share a hobby, talent, or information related to the concepts which are being stressed provides another meaningful way to help the children learn about energy. Some of the ways teachers can have parents participate in classroom activities are:

* Having a parent come and do exercises with the children
* Having a parent who is a coal miner, electrician or chef discuss his or her occupation with the children
* Inviting a parent to assist on a field trip

To further enhance the children's understanding of energy, concepts can be reinforced by the comments the teacher makes as situations arise spontaneously in the children's play and involvement in activities. Such comments might be:

* "Look how the wind is moving the tree branches."
* "Johnny, you're using a lot of energy to pedal your tricycle."
* "If you're cold, play in the sun. It will keep you warm."

This unit should provide enjoyable and meaningful experiences for young children when all of the different avenues for teaching suggested above are utilized. These teaching methods have been proven successful through the significant gains in energy knowledge exhibited by the preschool children exposed to this unit as part of the energy research project described in Appendix C.

I. ENERGY AWARENESS

A. ENERGY IS THE ABILITY TO DO WORK

Energy is defined as the ability to do work or to move something. Children can observe their own body energy through physical activity and the body heat which results from physical activity.

1. Discuss the concept that our bodies have warmth. Have the children run in place, march, shake, stomp, clap hands or do jumping jacks. Ask: "Do you feel warmer?" "Do you know what makes you feel warmer?" Introduce the term "body energy" to the children.

2. Have the children run on the playground or climb on an obstacle course on a cold day. Ask: "Do you feel warmer?" Initiate a discussion by saying, "Why do you feel warmer than you did before you began climbing?"

3. Play "Follow the Leader" with the teacher being the leader. After they have exerted themselves for four to five minutes, have the children sit down and discuss body temperature. Other possible activities to precede this discussion include dancing with streamers, doing football warm-up exercises, playing a circle game with a ball, throwing bean bags at cans, and walking the balance beam.

4. Play "Ring Around a Rosy." Comment on the energy being used while playing the game.

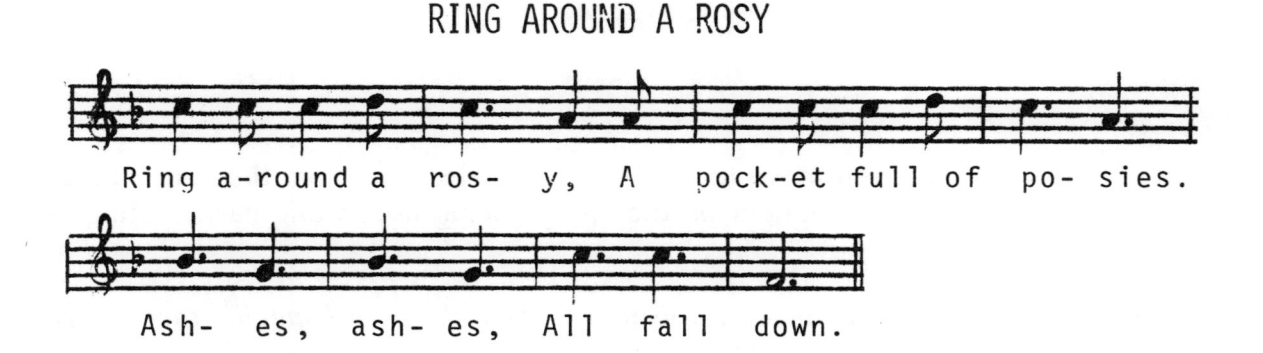

RING AROUND A ROSY

Ring a-round a ros-y, A pock-et full of po-sies.
Ash-es, ash-es, All fall down.

5. Have the children move to a selection or selections from The Children's Record Guild record *Nothing to Do.** Comment on the energy being used while participating in the activity.
6. Have the children move to a selection or selections from the Harold and Mary Jane LaCrone record *Physical Fitness for Preschool*. Comment on the energy being used while participating in the activity.

7. Have the children move to a selection or selections from the Hap Palmer record *Movin'*. Comment on the energy being used while participating in the activity.

*Many of the activities included in this unit involve the use of specific recordings, books, filmstrips, teaching kits, etc. In each case, only the name will be given in the text. For more complete information regarding the book, recording, etc., including the author's name and the publisher or manufacturer, see Appendix B.

8. Recite the finger play "Five Little Monkeys Jumping on the Bed." If you wish, use flannel characters to illustrate the story. Ask the children: "Does it take more energy for the monkeys to jump or stand still?" Discuss their answers. Then ask: "Do you think the monkeys feel warmer after they have been jumping or after they have been standing still?" Discuss these responses. Have the children stand. Ask: "Do you feel warm or cool? Why?" Have the children jump up and down like monkeys as you recite the words to the finger play. When finished, seat the children and ask: "Do you feel warmer now than before we started? Why?" Discuss their answers.

Five Little Monkeys

Five little monkeys jumping on the bed,
One fell off and bumped his head.
He called for the doctor; the doctor said,
"That's what you get for jumping on the bed."

Four little monkeys jumping on the bed,
(progress to no monkeys).

Flannel Board Pattern

9. On a rainy day, put a tumbling mat in the middle of the floor. As the children tumble, comment on the energy they are using.
10. As a group time activity, have the children one at a time dramatize a way they use body energy. Have the group of children guess what the child who is dramatizing is doing. Discuss how each child gets the energy to perform these activities. (Primarily for five year olds.)
11. Provide rhythm band instruments at music time. Play several selections with the children as they march about the room. Comment on the energy being used to play the instruments and march.
12. Play the singing game "Punchinello." Encourage the children to introduce activities that use a lot of energy.

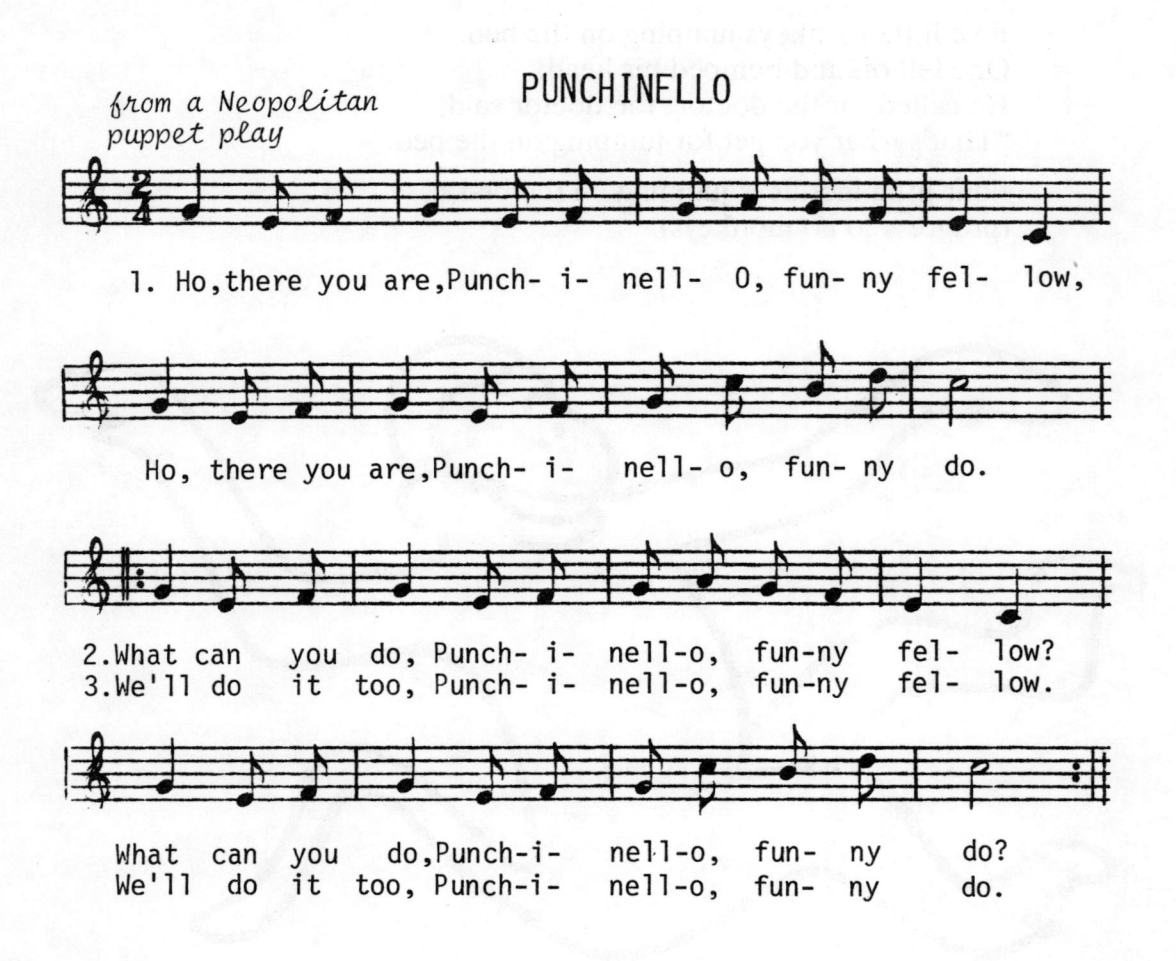

PUNCHINELLO

from a Neopolitan puppet play

1. Ho, there you are, Punch-i-nell-o, fun-ny fel-low,
   Ho, there you are, Punch-i-nell-o, fun-ny do.
2. What can you do, Punch-i-nell-o, fun-ny fel-low?
   What can you do, Punch-i-nell-o, fun-ny do?
3. We'll do it too, Punch-i-nell-o, fun-ny fel-low.
   We'll do it too, Punch-i-nell-o, fun-ny do.

B. ENERGY MAKES THINGS MOVE

Active or kinetic energy is energy in motion. People need energy to move. Machines also need energy to move. All moving things have a source of energy: trees have wind, people have food, cars have gasoline, and so forth.

1. Present familiar energy-using objects or facsimilies of them to the children. Examples are a toy automobile, a toaster, and an electric clock. Discuss the questions: "Why do you go to the gas station?" "What would happen if you didn't put gas in the car?" "Why do you plug it in?" "What would happen if you did not plug it in?"
2. Prepare a matching game of energy-users and their energy sources. Play the game with a small group of children as you would a lotto game or let individual children match the objects to their energy sources on their own.

Directions

On a large poster board, draw pictures similar to the ones above of the wind, sun, and water. Collect many different pictures from magazines of various energy-users which can be matched with the energy sources pictured on the poster. For example, in the illustration above, the sailboat would be placed under the wind. With a small group of children, call on one child at a time and use statements such as: "Place the picture of the sailboat under the kind of energy it needs to move." This activity may also be used by individual children as they match objects to sources on their own. The poster may be covered with clear contact paper for protection.

Directions

On a large poster board, draw pictures similar to the ones above of an electrical socket and plug, food, and gasoline pump. Collect many different pictures from magazines of various energy-users which can be matched with the energy sources pictured on the poster. For example, in the illustration above, the truck would be placed under the gasoline pump. With a small group of children, call on one child at a time and use statements such as "Place the picture of the truck under the kind of energy it needs to move." This activity may also be used by individual children as they match objects to sources on their own. The poster may be covered with clear contact paper for protection.

3. Using the Federal Energy Administration character, Energy Ant, make a game called "Energy Ant says feed me . . ." Prepare a large poster on cardboard of Energy Ant's face with the mouth opening cut out. Cut out magazine pictures of electrical appliances, appliances and vehicles that run on gas, oil, and coal, objects the wind moves, and objects the sun heats. Have the children feed these to Energy Ant as he, speaking through the teacher, requests them to do so with statements such as "Energy Ant says feed me something that the wind moves."

Directions

On a large poster board, draw a picture similar to the one above of Energy Ant's face with the mouth opening cut out. Collect many pictures from magazines of various energy-users to be "fed" to Energy Ant. Place a few pictures at a time on the floor or table in front of Energy Ant. Pretending to be Energy Ant's voice, have the children feed Energy Ant the various energy-users by making statements such as "Energy Ant says feed me something that uses gasoline energy." The poster may be covered with clear contact paper for protection.

4. Have the children throw balls and bean bags; comment on the concept that body movements use energy. Ask: "How do you know you have used energy?"

5. Sing the song "What Shall We Do?" with the children. Discuss the concept that energy helps people move. Have the children substitute words in the song for things they can do when they have a lot of energy.

WHAT SHALL WE DO?

Mary Jaye Game Song

1. What shall we do on a win-ter's day, Win-ter's day, win-ter's day? What shall we do on a win-ter's day, When we can't go out and play?

2. We'll play with toys on a win-ter's day, Win-ter's day, win-ter's day. We'll play with toys on a win-ter's day, when we can't go out and play.

3. I'm a steam shovel and I dig, dig, dig...
   I dig on a winter's day.
4. I'm a rocket shop and I zoom, zoom, zoom...
   I zoom on a winter's day.
5. I'm a spinning top and I whirl, whirl, whirl...
6. I'm a ballerina and I dance, dance, dance...
7. I'm a big robot and I walk, walk, walk...

Reprinted by permission from
Making Music Your Own K, by Mary
Jaye. Copyright 1966, Silver
Burdett Company.

C. ENERGY IS ALL AROUND US

There are many sources of energy: food, the sun, the wind, moving water and fossil fuels. Man uses these sources of energy to improve his way of living.

1. Show concrete examples of energy sources such as a piece of coal, a jar of oil, a water wheel, a model windmill and a model solar collector. Leave them out for the children to observe and discuss over a period of time.

2. In small groups take a tour of the school. Look for all of the pieces of equipment in the building that use energy, such as the furnace, electric lights, clocks, dishwasher, range, film projector, and so forth. Make a list of all the energy-users you find.

3. Generally discuss a variety of energy sources: fossil fuel, wind, solar, and electrical. Use pictures from magazines of these energy sources to stimulate discussion.

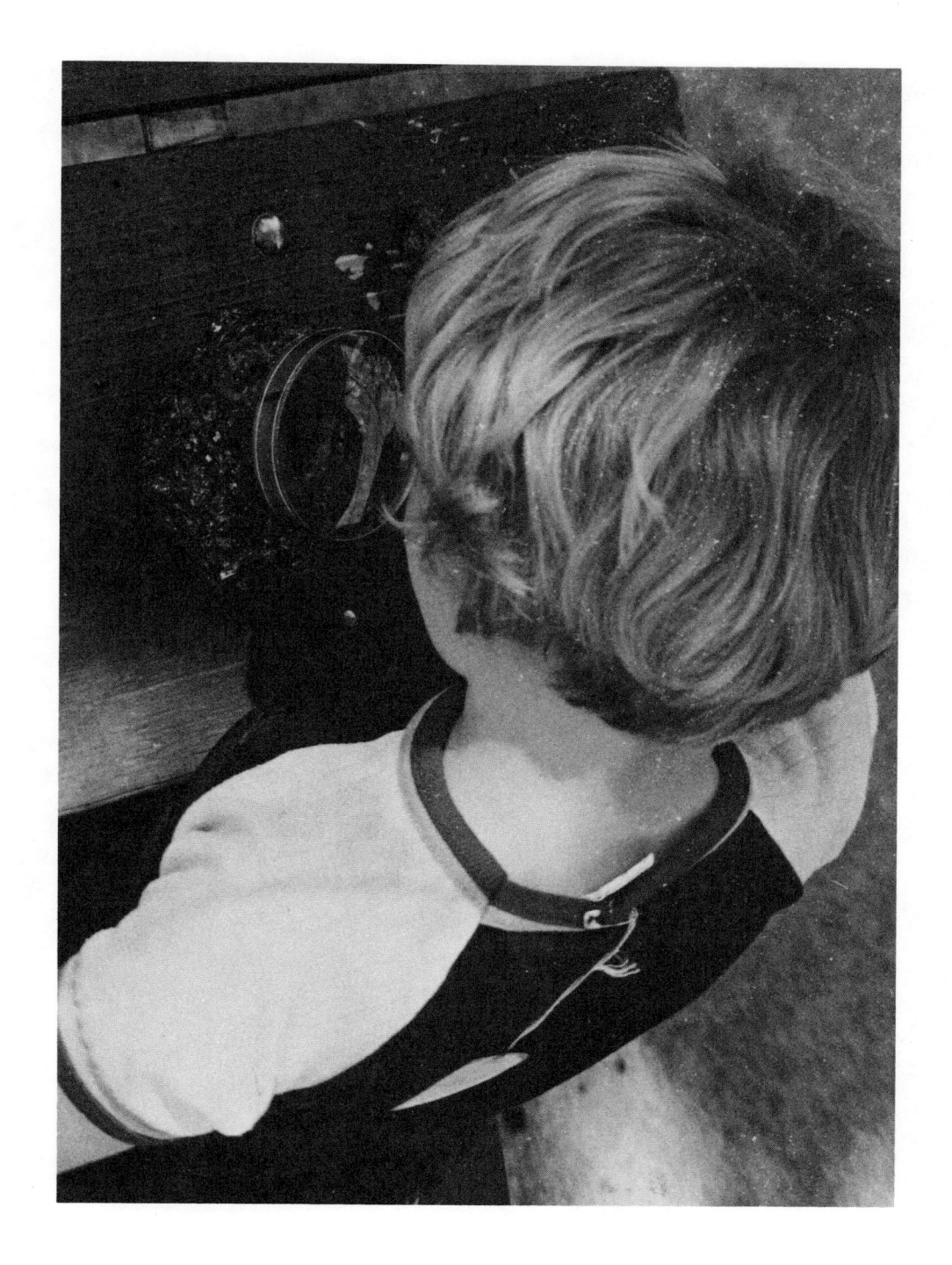

II. SOURCES OF ENERGY

A. OUR BODIES HAVE ENERGY

The energy that people need to do work, to move, and to keep warm comes from food. People take in energy daily in the form of food. This energy is stored in our bodies and is released as we need it.

1. OUR BODIES GET ENERGY FROM FOOD

  a. Discuss with the children the questions: "Why do we eat meals?" "What would happen if we didn't eat?" "How do you feel when you are sick?" "What must we do to get more energy?" Use pictures to stimulate the discussion.

  b. Discuss with the children the concept that natural sugars from fruits and vegetables give us energy. Make sure that the children understand that people who are strong eat a variety of foods. In a group, sample different fruits and vegetables.

  c. Read the story *Stone Soup* to the children. Have the children bring vegetables another day and tell the story as they make stone soup. Serve it at snack time with milk. Discuss eating foods from the basic four food groups.

  d. Have the children cut out pictures of food from magazines. Provide materials for them to make a collage of foods that give us energy.

  e. Set up a grocery store in the dramatic play area. Use empty food cartons, plastic fruits and plastic vegetables to stock the shelves. Have a cash register and play money for the children to use in purchasing the food, and paper bags for sacking the food. Allow the children to take their groceries to the home living area to "prepare" and "eat" to give their bodies energy.

  f. Tell the flannelboard story "Cheese, Peas, and Chocolate Pudding." Discuss with the children why it is important to eat a variety of foods.

Cheese, Peas, and Chocolate Pudding

There was once a little boy who ate cheese, peas, and chocolate pudding. Cheese, peas, and chocolate pudding. Cheese, peas, and chocolate pudding. Everyday the same old things, cheese, peas, and chocolate pudding.

For breakfast he would have some cheese. Any kind. Cream cheese, American cheese, Swiss cheese, Dutch cheese, Italian cheese, Blue cheese, Green cheese, Yellow cheese, Brick cheese. Even Liederkranz. Just cheese for breakfast.

For lunch he ate peas. Green or yellow peas. Frozen peas, canned peas, dried peas, split peas, black-eyed peas. No potatoes, though; just peas for lunch.

And for supper he would have cheese and peas, and chocolate pudding. Cheese, peas, and chocolate pudding. Cheese, peas, and chocolate pudding. Everyday the same old things, cheese, peas, and chocolate pudding.

Once his mother bought a lamb chop for him. She cooked it in a little frying pan on the stove, and she put some salt on it, and gave it to the little boy on a little blue dish. The boy looked at it. He smelled it. (It did smell delicious!) He even touched it. But . . .

"Is this cheese?" he asked.

"It's a lamb chop, darling," said his mother. The boy shook his head.

"Cheese!" he said. So his mother ate the lamb chop herself, and the boy had some cottage cheese.

One day his big brother was chewing a raw carrot. It sounded so good, the little boy reached his hand out for a bite.

"Sure!" said his brother. "Here!" The little boy almost put the carrot into his mouth, but at the last minute he remembered, and he said, "Is this peas?"

"No, fella, it's a carrot," said his brother.

"Peas," said the little boy firmly, handing the carrot back.

Once his daddy was eating a big dish of raspberry jello. It looked so shiny red and cool, the little boy came over and held his mouth open.

"Want a taste?" asked his daddy. The little boy looked and looked at the jello. He almost looked it off the dish but . . .

"Is it chocolate pudding?" he asked.

"No, son, it's jello," said his daddy. So the little boy frowned and backed away.

"Chocolate pudding!" he said.

His grandma baked cookies for him. "Nope!" said the boy.

His grandpa bought him an ice cream cone. The little boy just shook his head.

His aunt and uncle invited him for a fried chicken dinner. Everybody ate fried chicken and fried chicken and more fried chicken. Except the little boy. And you know what he ate.

Cheese, peas, and chocolate pudding. Cheese, peas, and chocolate pudding. Everyday the same old thing, cheese, peas, and chocolate pudding.

But one day—ah, one day a very funny thing happened. The little boy was playing puppy. He lay on the floor and growled and barked and rolled over. He crept to the table where his big brother was having lunch.

"Arf-arf!" he barked.

"Good doggie!" said his brother, patting his head. The little boy lay down on his back on the floor and barked again.

But at that minute, his big brother dropped a piece of something from his plate. And the little boy's mouth was just ready to say "Arf!" And what do you think happened?

Something dropped into the little boy's mouth. He sat up in surprise. Because something was on his tongue. And something was warm and juicy and delicious!

And it didn't taste like cheese. And it did not taste like peas. And it certainly wasn't chocolate pudding.

The little boy chewed slowly. Each chew tasted better than the last. He swallowed something and opened his mouth again. Wide. As wide as he could.

"Want some more?" asked his brother. The little boy closed his mouth and thought.

"That's not cheese," he said.

"No, it's not," said his brother.

"And it couldn't be chocolate pudding."

"No, it certainly is not chocolate pudding," smiled his brother. "It's hamburger." The little boy thought hard.

"I like hamburger," he said.

So his big brother shared the rest of his hamburger with the little boy, and ever after that, guess what?

Ever after that, the little boy ate cheese, peas, and chocolate pudding and hamburger.

Until he was your age, of course. When he was your age, he ate everything.

—Betty Van Witsen

FLANNEL BOARD PATTERNS

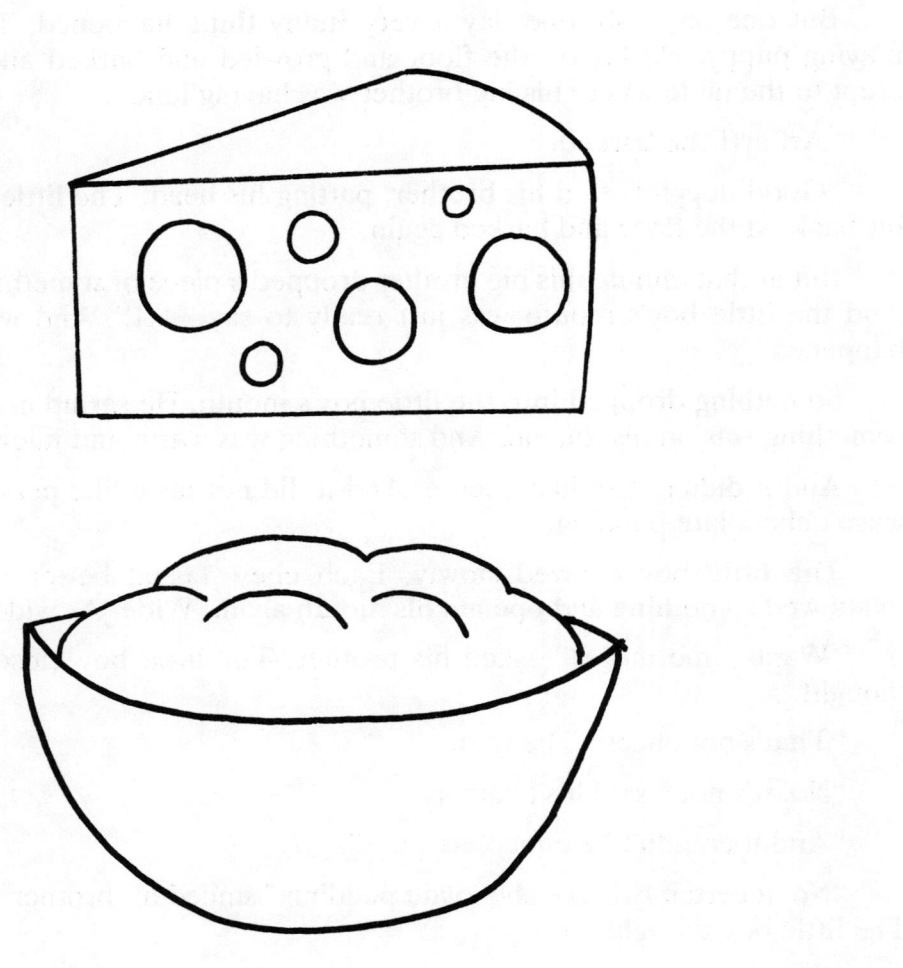

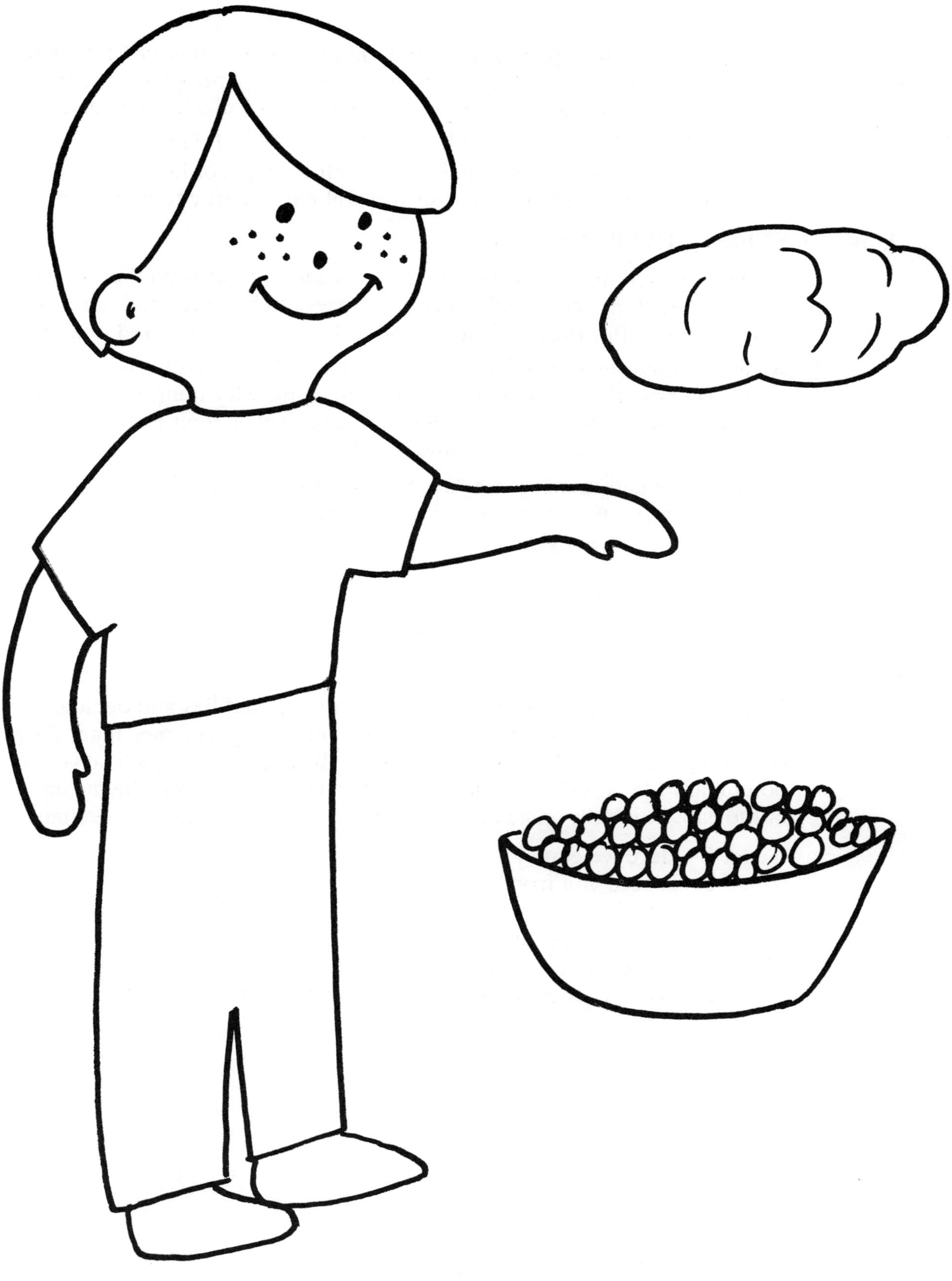

g. During outdoor free play, supply the children with a basket filled with plastic fruits and vegetables, empty food cartons, paper plates, utensils, and a blanket. As the children play out the role of picnic, comment on the energy they are getting from the food they are "eating."

h. Dismiss the children to wash their hands before snack or lunch by saying, "Mary, you may get ready to eat so you will have energy to play later."

2. BODY ENERGY HELPS US MOVE

a. During a group time, have the children (as a group) position their bodies the way they think they would look if they were sick, if they had not eaten properly, and after they had eaten a good breakfast, lunch, and dinner.

b. At group time, as the teacher narrates, have the children (as a group) dramatize how they look and feel when they are very hungry, how they look when they are eating, how they look and feel as their energy comes back, how they look and feel when they have lots of energy.

c. Play the pantomime game "Lemonade" to illustrate all the activities we can perform when we have a lot of energy.

Lemonade

Children are divided into two teams. Each team huddles and decides on something to act out for the other team. Team 1 approaches team 2 by beginning the chant. Teams alternate until the chant is complete at which point team 1 begins their pantomine. When team 2 discovers the meaning of the pantomine the game begins again with team 2 beginning the chant.

Team 1—Here we come!
Team 2—Where you from?
Team 1—New York!
Team 2—What's your trade?
Team 1—Lemonade.
Team 2—Well get to work and show us some if you're not afraid.

3. BODY ENERGY KEEPS US WARM
   a. On a cold day, have the children compare how warm they feel when they first go outside to how warm they feel after they have run and played for two to three minutes.
   b. Using pictures of people bicycling, jogging, playing games, and so forth, discuss with the children the idea that body energy keeps us warm.
   c. During group time, make a list with the children of all the things they can do on the playground to make themselves warm on a cold day.
   d. Read the poem "Shiver and Quiver."

Shiver and Quiver

When it's cold, you shiver and you quiver.
   B-r-r-r, b-r-r-r, b-r-r-r.
     (Clasp arms and shiver.)

When it's cold, you shiver and you quiver.
   B-r-r-r, b-r-r-r, b-r-r-r

Your hands feel just like ice
   (Rub hands vigorously.)

So you rub them once or twice.
When it's cold, you shiver and you quiver.
   B-r-r-r, b-r-r-r, b-r-r-r!

Reprinted by permission from *Let's Do Fingerplays,* by Marion Grayson. Copyright, 1962, Robert B. Luce, Inc., Bethesda, Maryland

B. WE GET ENERGY FROM THE SUN

The sun is the source of almost all energy. Energy from the sun is called heat energy. Heat energy can be stored for later use. Green plants store the sun's energy. People and animals eat plants to get energy. Heat energy can also be stored in mechanical devices such as solar collectors and used later to heat homes. The energy available from the sun is unlimited.

1. ENERGY FROM THE SUN IS CALLED HEAT ENERGY

   a. Have the children put a piece of black construction paper in a sunny place. Leave it for one hour. Have the children touch it. Ask: "What has happened?" "Why is it hot?" Discuss solar heat.
   b. Have the children put a black pan filled with cold water in the sun. Measure the water temperature with a thermometer and record it on paper. Go back in an hour and measure the temperature again. Ask: "What has happened?" "Why is it warmer?" Discuss solar heat.

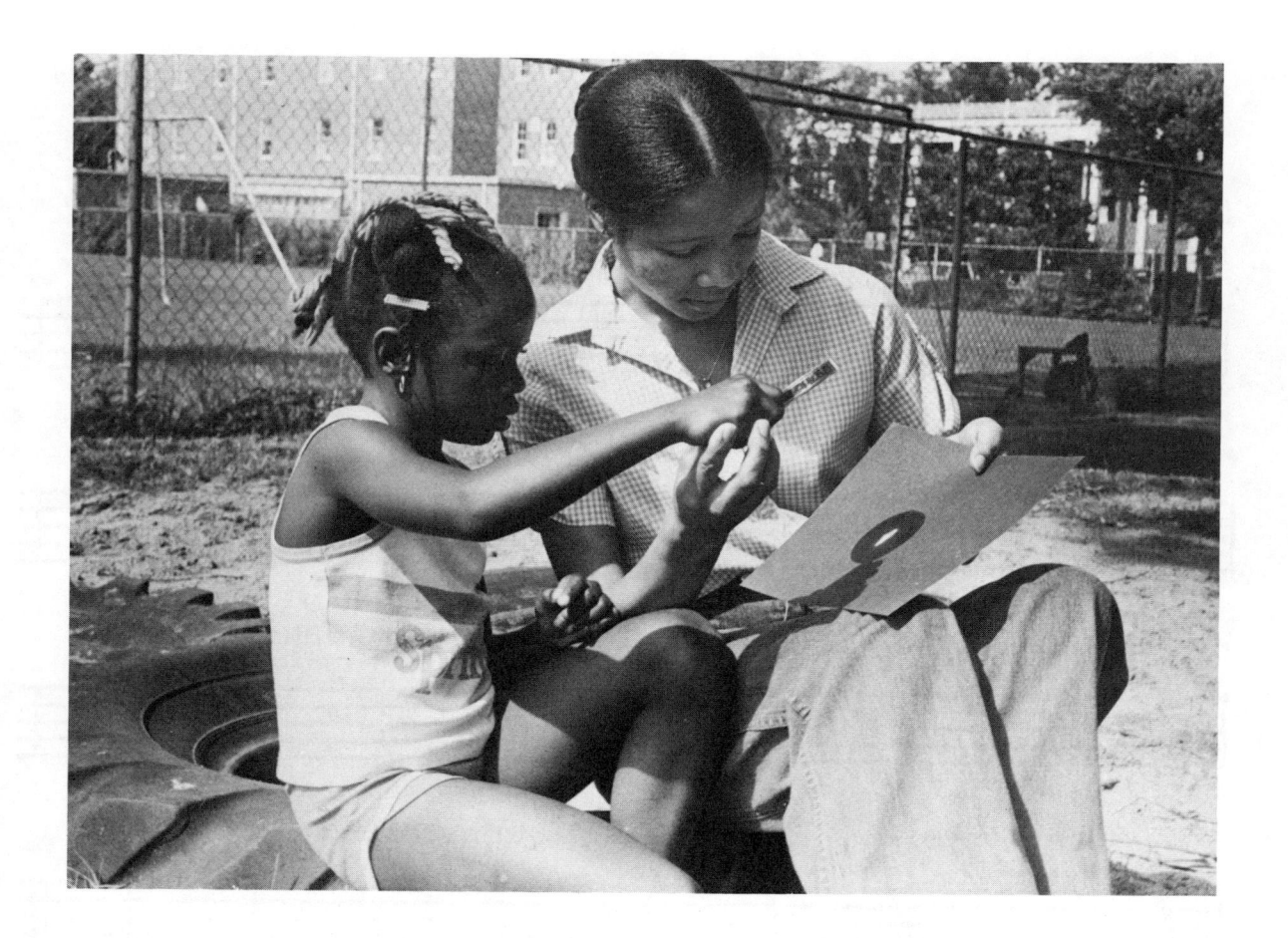

c. Outside, place a piece of paper on the ground. Hold a magnifying glass at an angle over the paper, but close to the paper, so that the sun shines through the magnifying glass onto the paper. In a very short time the paper will smolder. Discuss the heat we get from the sun. (It is well to practice this experiment before trying it with children.)

d. Read the book *The Day We Saw the Sun Come Up* to the children.

e. Read the book *Sunlight* to the children.

f. Read the book *The Day the Sun Danced* to the children.

g. As a group, paint pictures of a sunny day. Provide clear bright colors and large sheets of paper.

h. At music time sing, "The Sun." Discuss how a sunny day makes you feel.

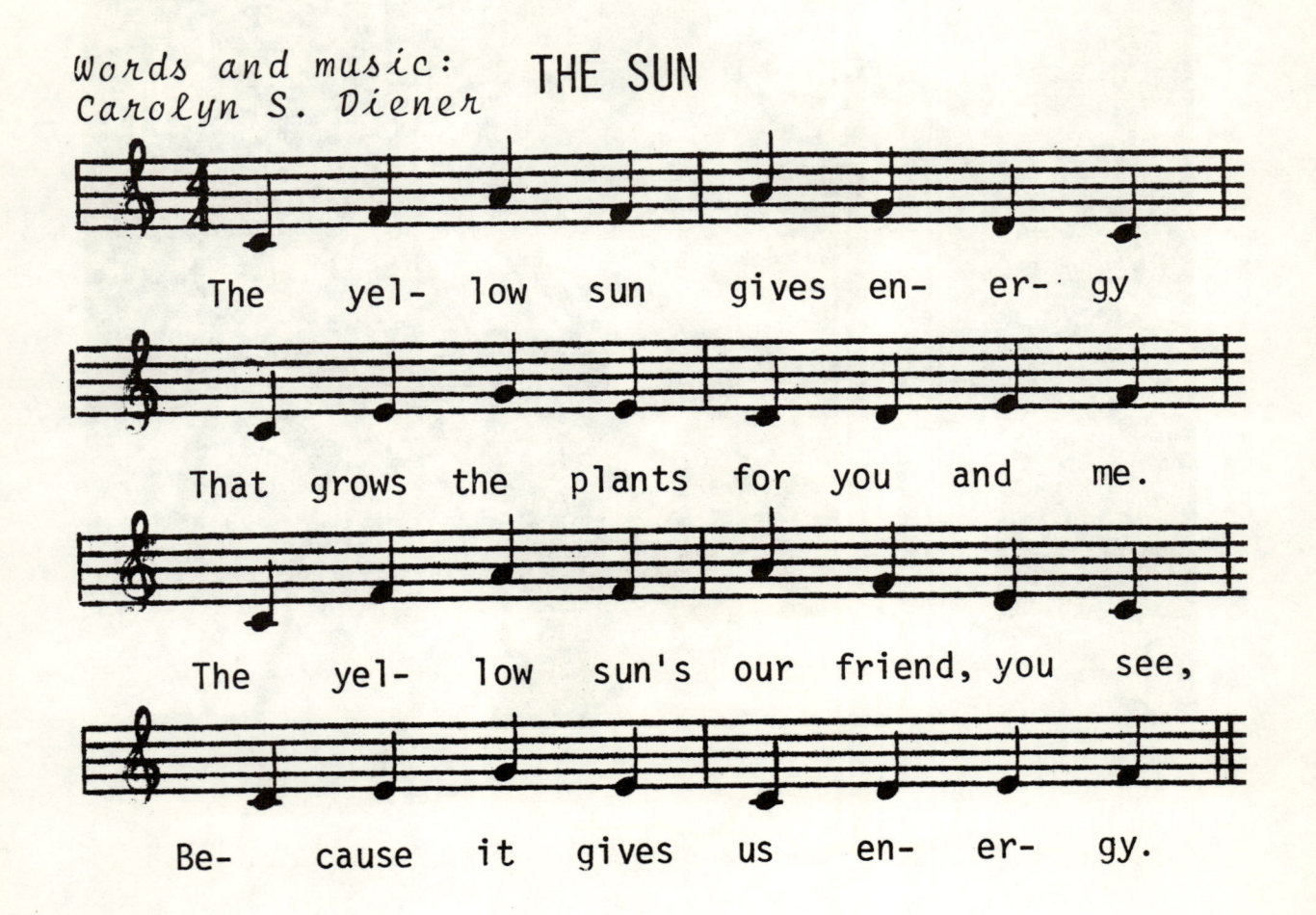

Words and music: Carolyn S. Diener

THE SUN

The yel- low sun gives en- er- gy

That grows the plants for you and me.

The yel- low sun's our friend, you see,

Be- cause it gives us en- er- gy.

2. **HEAT ENERGY WARMS OUR BODIES**

a. Compare air temperature in a sunny spot and a shady spot using two thermometers. Have the children keep a daily record of both. Discuss the results after a week.

b. Have the children compare the perceived temperature by sitting by a sunny window and sitting in a shaded part of the same room. Discuss their perceptions with them.

3. HEAT ENERGY CAN BE COLLECTED IN AN ENCLOSED SPACE SUCH AS A TANK OR A CAN

a. Have each child bring from home two empty one pound coffee cans with plastic lids. The teacher will paint all the cans with flat black spray paint. Make certain the child has his name on both cans. Put one can away. Have the children cap the remaining can. Place the cans one on top of the other in a sunny window. Have the children feel the heat radiating from them on a sunny day. Place a thermometer next to them and one in a distant part of the room. Have the children keep a temperature chart, comparing temperatures.

Directions

Write or have the children write their names on masking tape and put on the lids of their own coffee cans. Place the cans on their sides in rows. Use masking tape to hold them together. Place the rows on top of each other. Each row should have one fewer can than the row below it to allow more exposure to the sun.

b. Show the children models or pictures of solar heated homes and buildings. Explain how the solar collector works. Compare the one you made in the previous exercise to those in the pictures.

c. Take the children on a field trip to a solar heated building. Observe the collectors and the interior temperature.

4. HEAT ENERGY CAN BE COLLECTED IN WATER

a. Have the children take the remaining black coffee cans, fill these cans with water, and set them upright in a sunny window. Are the results the same as with the first set of coffee cans?

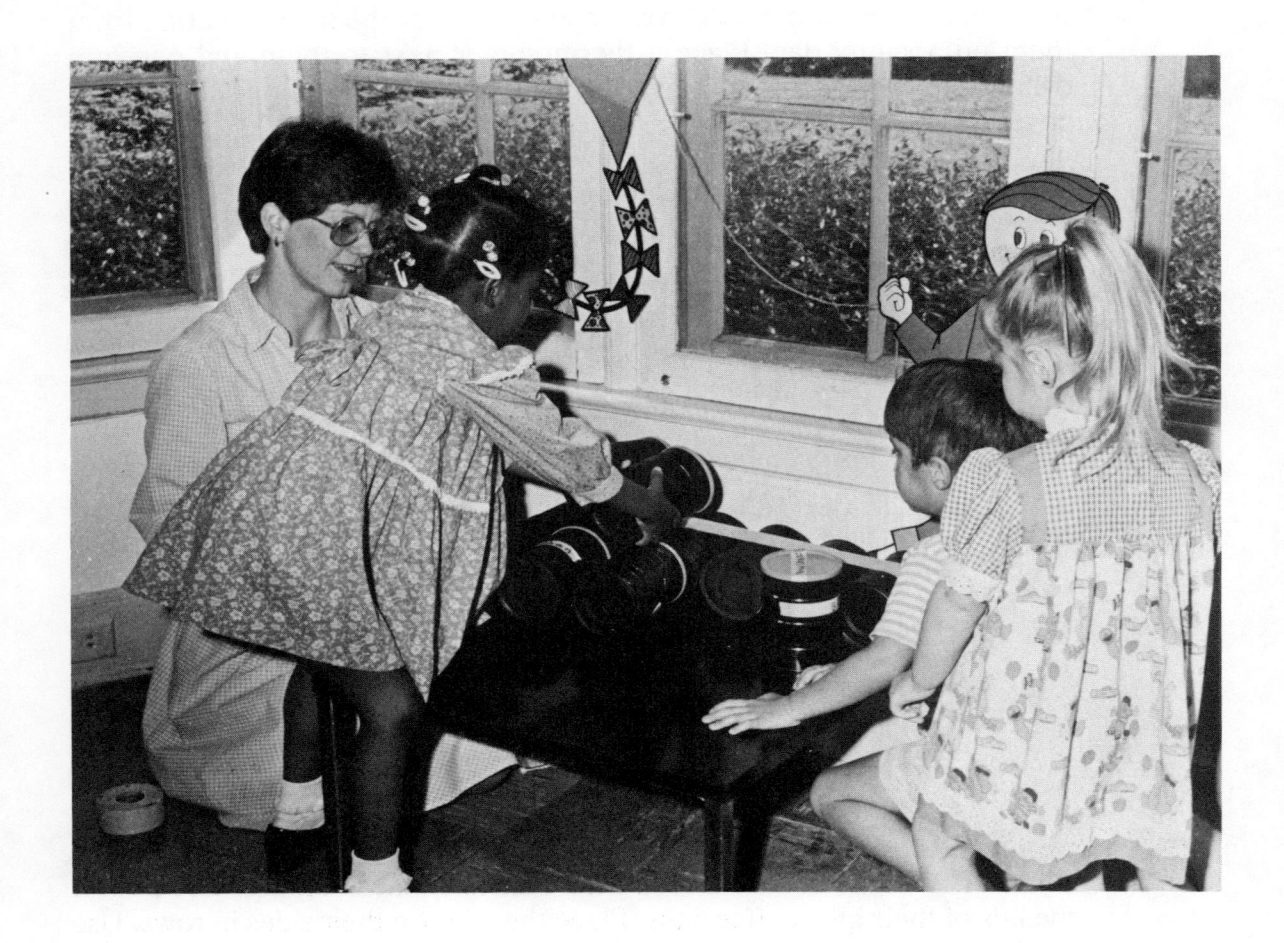

b. Have the children wash dishes or doll clothes in water heated by the sun.

c. Have the children hang half of the doll clothes in the sun and half of the doll clothes in the shade to dry. Compare how quickly each set dries.

C. WE GET ENERGY FROM THE WIND

The surface of the earth is covered by a layer of air. The movement of this air is called wind. People can feel the air moving. Sometimes the movement is gentle and sometimes the movement is strong. People have learned to use the wind to do work; for instance, people use wind to move boats with sails and to turn windmills that can pump water or generate electricity.

1. WIND IS MOVING AIR

  a. Have the children tie crepe paper streamers to an outside support such as a fence or mailbox. Observe when and how much they move. Ask: "What makes them move?" "What other things does the wind move?"
  b. Have the children make wind chimes to hang outside. Notice when the wind blows them hard enough to make a noise.

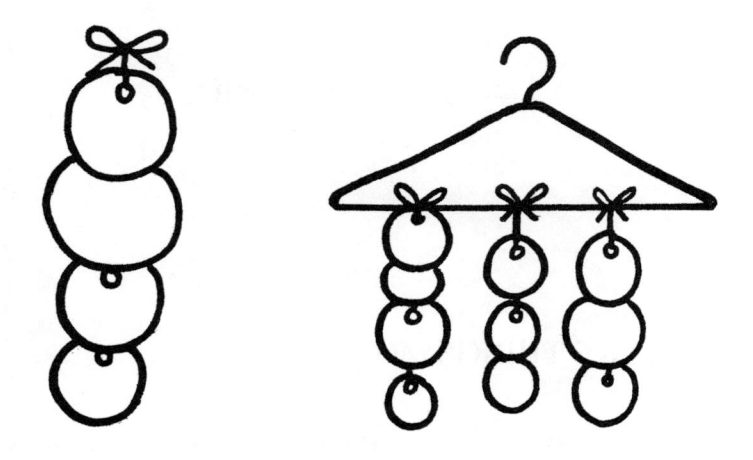

Directions

Use jar lids or sea shells to make wind chimes. Make a hole in each so that the children may string them together. Have the children tie several strings of lids or shells to a coat hanger so that they will hit together in the wind.

c. While the other children observe, have a child run closely by the crepe paper streamers. Do the streamers move when he passes them? Discuss why. Repeat the same experiment with the wind chimes.
  d. At music time, have the children dance with scarves. Ask them to make their scarves move like a soft breeze, a strong wind, the North wind and so forth.
  e. On a windy day, let balloons go free on an open field. Have the children try to catch them.
  f. At music time, have the children bat balloons with paper wands or their hands while listening to music that varies in tempo like the wind.
  g. Read the poem "The Wind is Moving Air."

The Wind Is Moving Air

The wind is moving air,
Ooh, ooh.
It moves things here and there,
It makes balloons dance way up high,
It keeps kites flying in the sky,
The wind is moving air.
Ooh, ooh.

—Carmen Jettinghoff

2. WIND CAN MAKE THINGS MOVE

  a. Using mural paper to record their responses, have the children dictate a list of all the objects they have observed the wind moving, such as leaves, branches, grass, paper, flags, and utility wires. Paste magazine pictures of the objects on the mural. Hang the mural. (Primarily for five year olds.)
  b. Get a kite up in the air. Let the children feel the strength of the wind pulling it. Discuss how strong the wind is.

c. Make pinwheels with the children. Have them take the pinwheels outside and experiment with getting them to move.

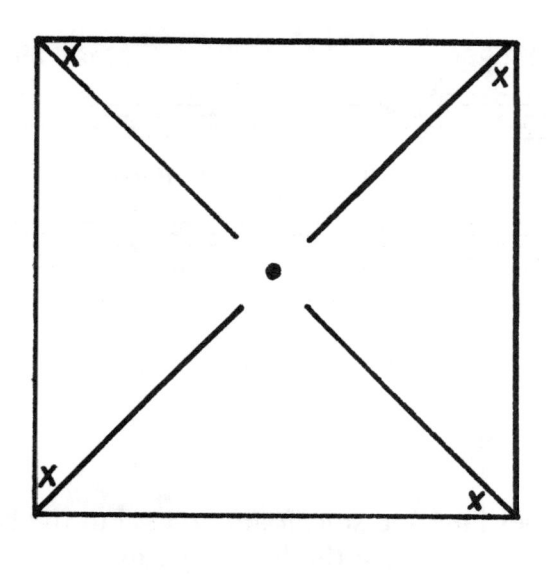

Directions

Use a square piece of construction paper approximately nine inches by nine inches. Draw lines from each corner to approximately 1/2" from the dot in the center of the paper, as shown in the illustration. Cut lines. Turn every other corner (as marked with the "x" in the illustration) to the center dot. Stick a straight pin through all the turned down corners at the center dot and then through a plastic straw. Bend the sharp point of the pin down, allowing enough room for play, and cover with masking tape. The children may color the paper for their pinwheels before they are made by the teacher.

d. Read *The Storm Book*. Discuss the action of the wind in the book. Discuss what other things the wind can move.

e. At music time, sing and act out the song, "Like A Leaf."

LIKE A LEAF

Unknown — Folk Tune

Like a leaf or a feath-er In the wind-y, wind-y weath-er, We will whirl a-round & twirl a-round & all fall down to- geth- er.

f. With the children, make paper fans and styrofoam boats. Put the boats in the water table. Have the children move the boats by fanning them with the paper fans or by directly blowing on them.

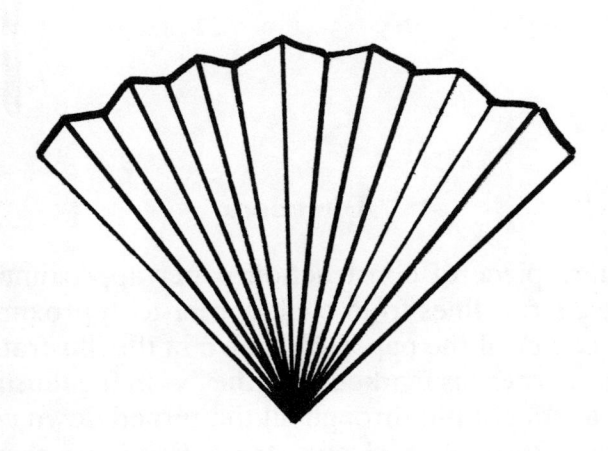

Directions

Fold a piece of drawing paper back and forth several times. Tape at one end and spread open to make a fan. Children may color the paper before it is folded by the teacher.

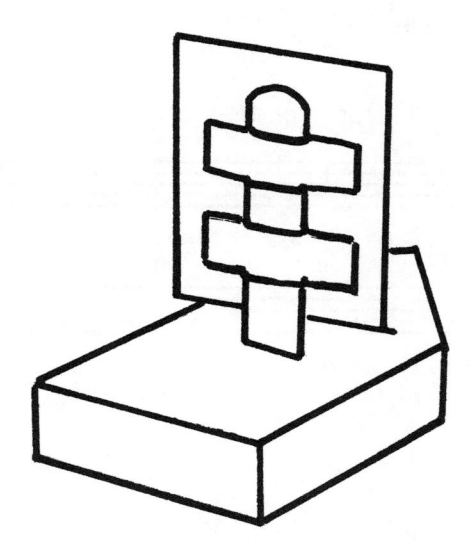

Directions

Cut out the shape for the boat from styrofoam. Use construction paper for the sail. Children may color the sails for their boats. Attach the sail to a popsicle stick or tongue depressor with masking tape and insert in the boat.

g. Make paper kites with the children. Have the children pull the kites after themselves as they run on the playground.

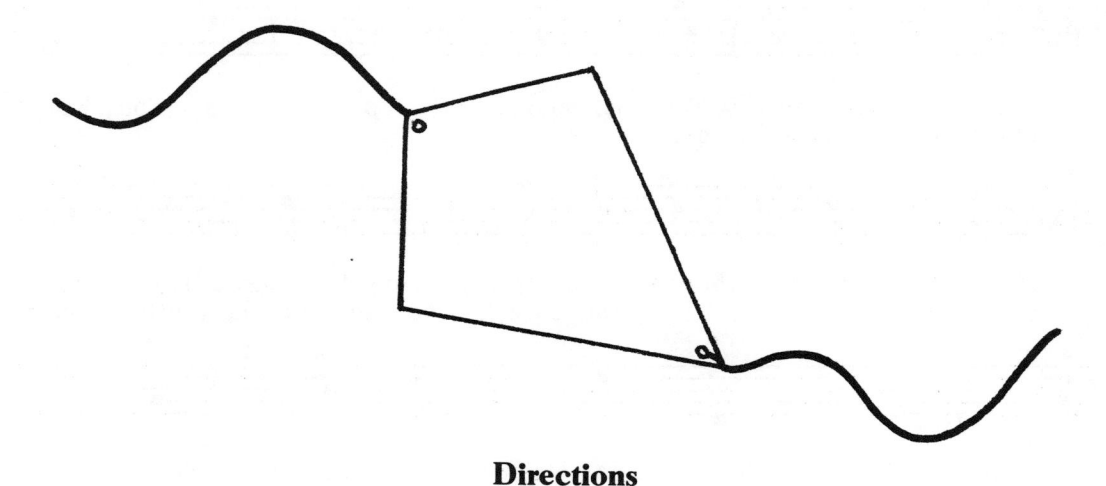

Directions

Cut a piece of drawing paper or construction paper into the shape of a kite. Children may color the paper for their own kites. Punch a hole at the top of the kite and tie a piece of string through the hole to pull the kite with. Punch another hole at the bottom of the kite and tie a piece of yarn through it for the tail.

h. At music time, sing "The Trees."

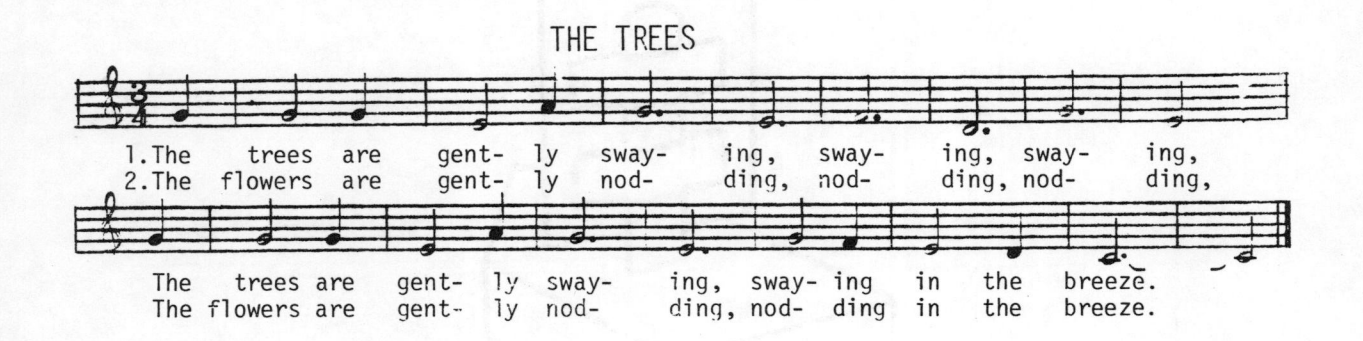

THE TREES

1. The trees are gent-ly sway-ing, sway-ing, sway-ing,
   The trees are gent-ly sway-ing, sway-ing in the breeze.
2. The flowers are gent-ly nod-ding, nod-ding, nod-ding,
   The flowers are gent-ly nod-ding, nod-ding in the breeze.

i. At music time, sing "The North Wind."

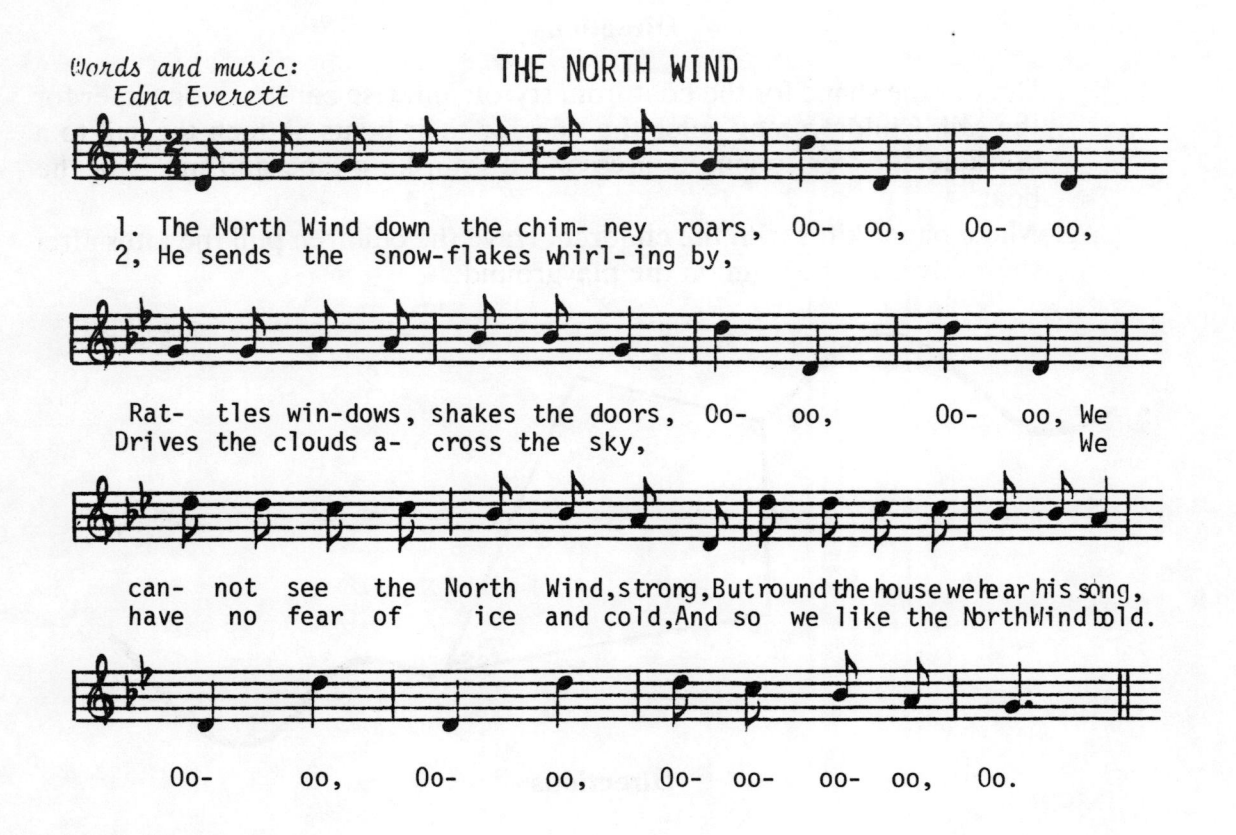

THE NORTH WIND

Words and music: Edna Everett

1. The North Wind down the chim-ney roars, Oo-oo, Oo-oo,
   Rat-tles win-dows, shakes the doors, Oo-oo, Oo-oo, We can-not see the North Wind, strong, But round the house we hear his song,
2. He sends the snow-flakes whirl-ing by,
   Drives the clouds a-cross the sky, We have no fear of ice and cold, And so we like the North Wind bold.

Oo-oo, Oo-oo, Oo-oo-oo-oo, Oo.

Reprinted by permission from
Making Music Your Own K, by Mary
Jaye. Copyright 1966, Silver
Burdett Company.

j. Read the book *Follow the Wind* to the children.

k. Read the book *Gilberto and the Wind* to the children.

l. At music time, sing "The Wind Blew East." Let the children make up new word combinations to fit the song.

THE WIND BLEW EAST

Traditional

The wind blew east, oo- oo, Oo- oo, The wind blew west, oo- oo, Oo- oo, Oh, the wind blew the sun- shine* right down to town. Oh, the

*Children may substitute other kinds of weather for sunshine.

m. Have the children blow bubbles outside. Observe with the children how the air catches the bubbles and carries them.

D. WE GET ENERGY FROM MOVING WATER

Much of the surface of the earth is covered by a layer of water. Flowing water has force; this force can be used to do work. In the past people used flowing water to turn large wheels on mills that ground grains into flour and meal.

1. WATER CAN BE USED TO MOVE THINGS

a. Bring a toy water wheel to group time. Have the children guess what it is and how it works. Put the water wheel in the water table and let the children experiment with it.

b. If possible, walk to a stream and observe the water flowing in it. Float styrofoam boats in the stream. Initiate discussion by saying, "The boats float downstream. Do you know why?"

c. On a warm day, use the water under pressure from a garden hose to sweep sand and leaves off the walk. Have the children try it.

d. Have two children stand at one end of the water table and agitate the water with manual egg beaters. Place styrofoam boats in the water. Discuss with the children what happens to the boats in the water.

e. Read the book *Curious George Rides a Bike* to the children.

f. At music time, sing, "Row, Row, Row Your Boat" and "The Allee Allee O!"

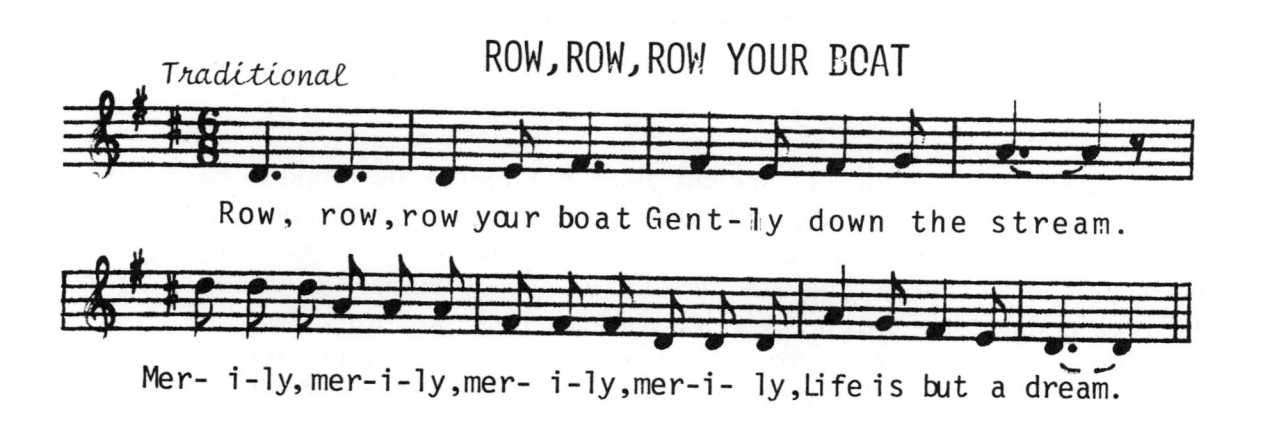

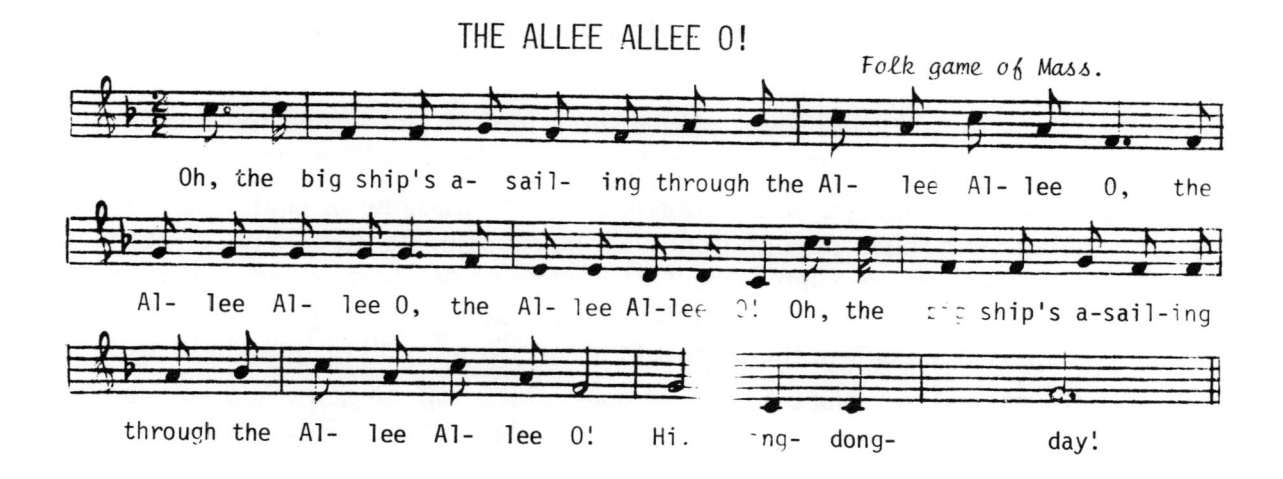

ROW, ROW, ROW YOUR BOAT
Traditional

Row, row, row your boat Gent-ly down the stream.

Mer-i-ly, mer-i-ly, mer-i-ly, mer-i-ly, Life is but a dream.

THE ALLEE ALLEE O!
Folk game of Mass.

Oh, the big ship's a-sail-ing through the Al-lee Al-lee O, the Al-lee Al-lee O, the Al-lee Al-lee O! Oh, the big ship's a-sailing through the Al-lee Al-lee O! Hi-ng-dong-day!

E. WE GET ENERGY FROM FOSSIL FUELS

Fossils are the remains of ancient plant and animal life found in earth, rock, and clay. Some fossils are imprints of the plant or animal that made them. Other fossils such as coal, oil and natural gas are fuels. Fossil fuels are mined by people for use as an energy source. This energy is stored energy which is given off when the fuel is burned. Most of the energy which is released is in the form of heat.

Coal is found under the ground in solid form. It is mined and then transported by truck, barge or train to the place where it will be stored or burned.

Oil is found under the ground and sea in liquid form. It is collected by drilling a deep well into the ground and pumping it out. It is then transported by pipe lines or oil tankers to the place where it will be stored or burned. Oil can be converted to gasoline. Both oil and gasoline are burned in vehicles.

Natural gas is a mixture of gases found under the ground. It is collected and transported much the same way that oil is. Natural gas is frequently burned in home furnaces and ranges.

1. COAL, OIL AND NATURAL GAS ARE FOSSIL FUELS

a. Show the children fossils. Have them look at and touch the imprint of organic matter in the rock, such as ferns, shells and insects.

b. Take the children on a field trip to see a large pile of coal. Back in the classroom, have the children describe the trip. As they do so, print their descriptions on a large sheet of newsprint or chart paper. When each child has made his or her contribution, read the children's "story" of their experience back to them. Post the "story" on a wall or bulletin board.

c. At group time, place a piece of coal, a jar of oil, an empty gas can, and a small propane tank in a row visible to the children. Have them identify discuss each of the items. Cover them with a blanket. Take one away without the children seeing which one. Ask the children to identify which object is gone. Repeat with the other items.

2. FOSSIL FUELS ARE FOUND UNDER THE GROUND

   a. Show the children pictures of coal mines, miners and mining equipment, and pieces of coal. Discuss how coal is extracted from the ground.
   b. Show the children pictures of oil wells, well drillers, drilling equipment, and a jar of oil. Discuss how oil is extracted from the ground.
   c. Take the children on a field trip to a strip mine. Back in the classroom, have the children describe their trip. As they do so, print their descriptions on a large sheet of newsprint or chart paper. When each child has made his or her contribution, read the children's "story" of their experience back to them. Post the "story" on a wall or bulletin board.
   d. Bury some pieces of coal in the sand box. Have the children dig for them during outside playtime. Wear hard hats and pretend it is a coal mine.
   e. Show the children replicas of gasoline-run vehicles such as an automobile, a truck, an airplane, and a tractor. Ask the children: "What makes these vehicles move?" Show them a jar of gasoline. Ask: "What is gasoline made from?" Show them a jar of oil. Ask: "Where does oil come from?" Show them a picture of an oil well extracting oil from the ground. Discuss in simple terms the way an oil well works.

3. FOSSIL FUELS MUST BE BURNED TO MAKE ENERGY

   a. Outside, demonstrate to the children how to fill the tank on a camp heater, lantern, or stove and how to use them.
   b. Show the children the furnace at the school. Discuss how a furnace works.
   c. Have each child find out what fuel the heating system in his house uses. Make a list and put it on the wall or bulletin board.
   d. Take the children on a field trip to a power-generating station. Back in the classroom, have the children describe the trip. As they do so, print their descriptions on a large sheet of newsprint or chart paper. When each child has made his or her contribution, read the children's "story" of their experience back to them. Post the "story" on a wall or bulletin board.
   e. At group time, use a propane camp stove to pop popcorn. Serve it for a snack.

f. At music time, sing "The Little Red Caboose."

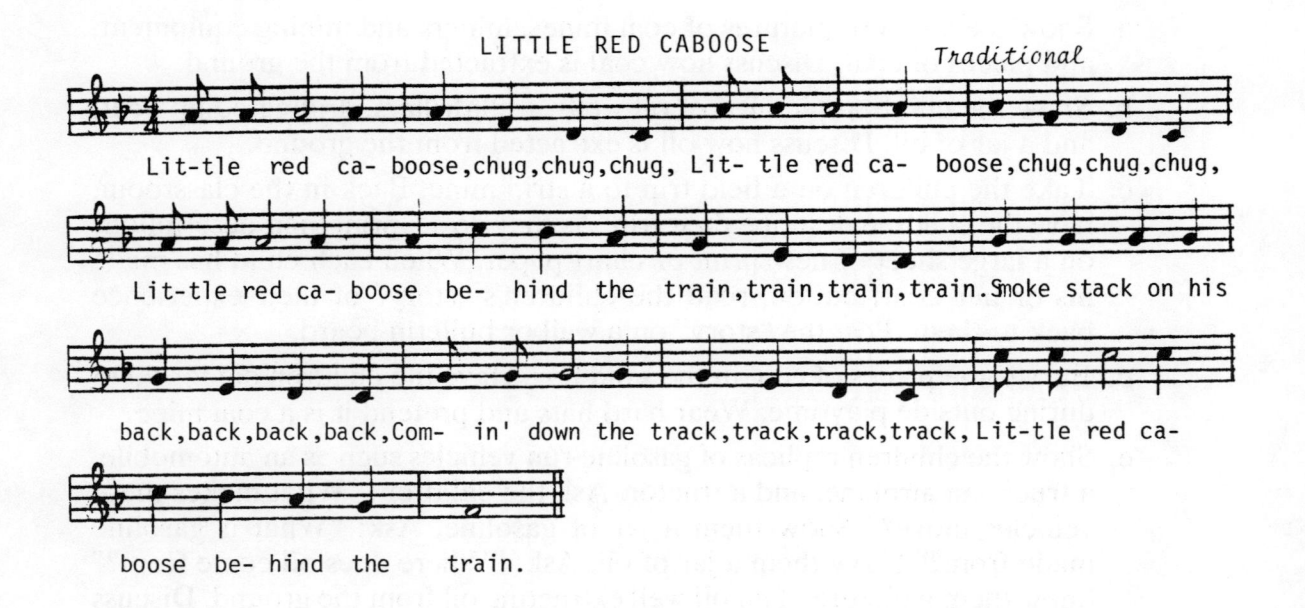

LITTLE RED CABOOSE
Traditional

Lit-tle red ca-boose, chug, chug, chug, Lit-tle red ca-boose, chug, chug, chug, Lit-tle red ca-boose be-hind the train, train, train, train. Smoke stack on his back, back, back, back, Com-in' down the track, track, track, track, Lit-tle red ca-boose be-hind the train.

g. At music time, sing "We're Going to the City."

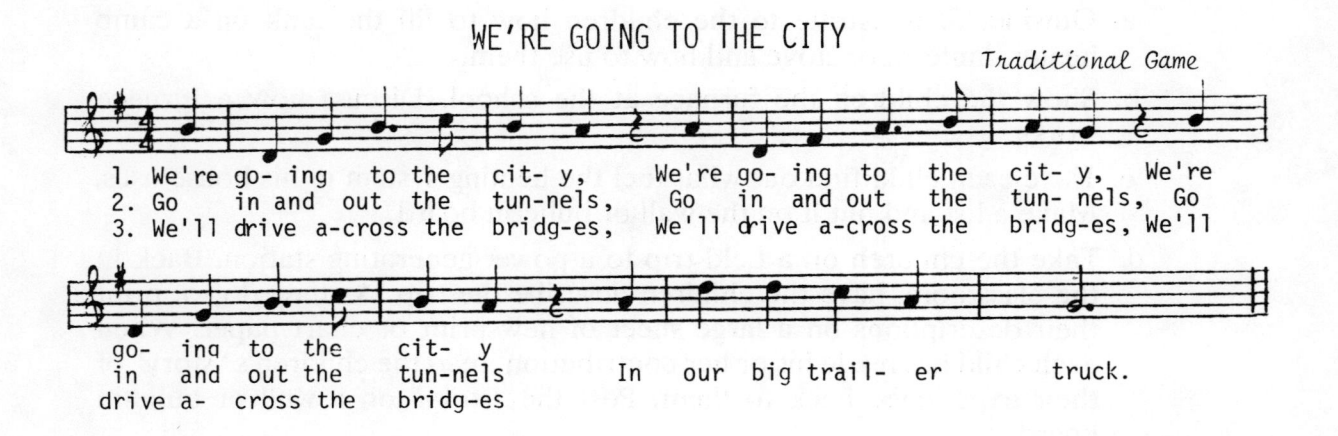

WE'RE GOING TO THE CITY
Traditional Game

1. We're go-ing to the cit-y, We're go-ing to the cit-y, We're go-ing to the cit-y
2. Go in and out the tun-nels, Go in and out the tun-nels, Go in and out the tun-nels
3. We'll drive a-cross the bridg-es, We'll drive a-cross the bridg-es, We'll drive a-cross the bridg-es

In our big trail-er truck.

Reprinted by permission from
Making Music Your Own K, by Mary
Jaye. Copyright 1966, Silver
Burdett Company.

h. At music time, sing "Let's Take a Little Trip."

LET'S TAKE A LITTLE TRIP

Words and music: Lolly Williams
Verse 3: Imagene Hilyard
Arr.: Georgette LeNorth

1. Let's take a lit-tle trip. Shall we board a train? We will trav-el miles & miles O-ver hill and plain. Woo! Woo! The whis-tle blows, Woo! Woo! A-way! Good-bye! Good-bye! We'll be back some day.

2. Let's take a lit-tle trip. Would you like to fly? We will take an As-tro-jet, Zoom-ing through the sky. Up! Up! In-to the air, Up! Up! A-way! Good-bye! Good-bye! We'll be back some day.

Verse 3.
Let's take a little trip. Would you like to sail?
We will board a big steamship, Hear the foghorns wail.
Sail! Sail! across the sea, Sail! Sail! away!
Good-by! Good-by! We'll be back some day.

Reprinted by permission from *Making Your Own K,* by Mary Jaye. Copyright 1966, Silver Burdett Company.

i. Tell the story *Chug-Along and Zoom* using flannel pieces or magazine pictures to depict the two automobiles. Discuss the fuel used by the two automobiles.

Chug-Along and Zoom*

(In this story the old car says, "Chug-along, chug-along, chug, chug, chug." The new car says, "Zoom!" When the story says, "The old car said," make the sound of the old car. When the story says, "The new car said," make that sound. Change the speed with which you make the sound according to what is happening in the story.)

Once there was a very old car. When it went down the road it said, "Chug-along, chug-along, chug, chug, chug." There was also a new car. When it went down the road it said, "Zoom!"

Every day the old car went down Skillmans' Lane. When it went up the hill it said slowly, "Chug-along, chug-along, chug, chug, chug." When it went down a hill it said, a little faster, "Chug-along, chug-along, chug, chug, chug."

Every day the new car went down Skillmans' Lane. When it went up a hill it said fast, "Zoom!" When it went down a hill it said fast, "Zoom!" It always went as fast as the law allowed.

Every day the new car and the old car parked side by side in a company parking lot.

"You go too fast on Skillmans' Lane," commented the old car one day when work was over. "Skillmans' Lane is very bumpy. Skillmans' Lane has many curves. You should slow down on Skillmans' Lane."

"Axle grease!" sneered the new car. "I am a new car. You are an old car. I can take bumps. I can take curves. I like to go as fast as the law allows. Good-bye now!" He left the parking lot saying, "Zoom!"

"Good-bye," called the old car. He left the parking lot saying, "Chug-along, chug-along, chug, chug, chug."

Now Skillmans' Lane was a country road. It was always bumpy. In summer and fall it was bumpy and dusty. In winter it was bumpy and snowy. In spring it was bumpy and muddy—very, very muddy, slishy, slashy, slide-around muddy—and it was full of holes.

---

*From *Listen and Help Tell the Story*, by Bernice Wells Carlson. Copyright © 1965 by Abingdon Press. Used by permission.

In the spring the old car went down Skillmans' Lane very carefully, dodging holes, going slowly over the bumps, and making sure not to get its wheels in the soft mud at the side of the road. It kept saying, "Chug-along, chug-along, chug, chug, chug."

The new car paid no attention to the mud. It went up the hill saying, "Zoom!" It started down the hill saying, "Zoom—Bang!" It hit a bump, swerved into the mud, and slid into a tree.

The old car heard the crash. It hurried up the hill as fast as it could go safely saying, "Chug-along, chug-along, chug, chug, chug."

"Stay where you are," called the old car. "I'll get a wrecker to pull you out." Off he went saying, "Chug-along, chug-along, chug, chug, chug."

The wrecker pulled the new car onto the road. It was a sad sight. It was all covered with mud; its headlights were broken; its fenders were bent. However, its engine was still running. "Oh, thank you, little old car. Thank you, wrecker. I think I can go on." He started down the road saying, slowly, "Z-o-o-m."

The cars still go down Skillmans' Lane. The old car says, "Chug-along, chug-along, chug, chug, chug." Sometimes it goes very slowly saying, "Chug-along, chug-along, chug, chug, chug." Sometimes it goes a little faster saying, "Chug-along, chug-along, chug, chug, chug." It all depends upon the condition of the road.

The nearly new car goes down Skillmans' Lane. Sometimes it goes slowly saying, "Z-o-o-m." Sometimes it goes a little faster saying, "Zoom!" Everything depends upon the condition of the road.

Flannel Board Pattern

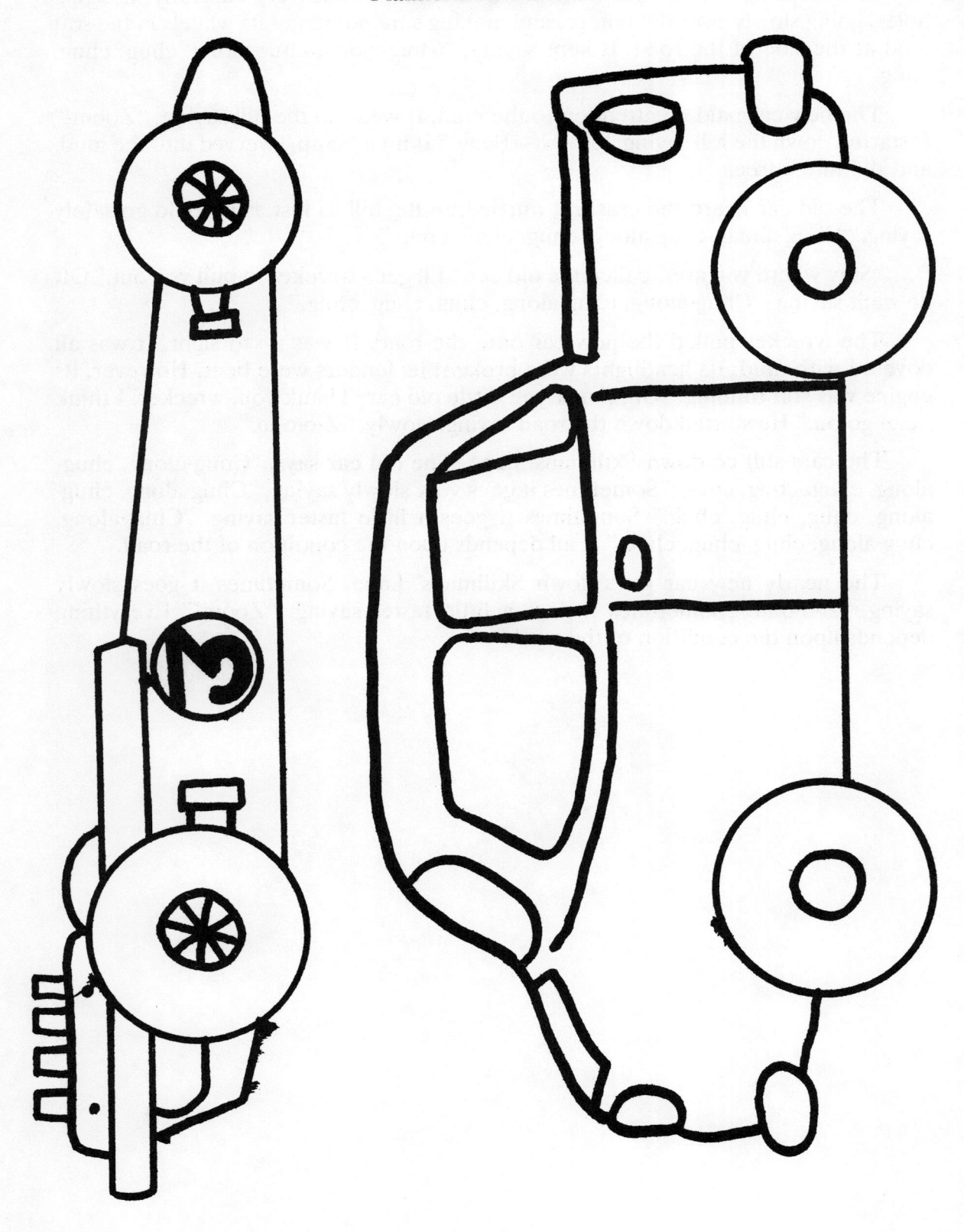

48

III. USES OF ENERGY

A. WE CAN USE OUR BODIES TO DO WORK

People use their own body energy to do work. Children can observe their own body energy being used to do work.

1. Let the children take turns winding a clock, using a manual can opener, spinning a top, and moving objects from one place to another. Discuss the fact that they have done work with their bodies. Where did the energy come from?
2. Have each child in the class bring a wind-up toy from home. Sit in a circle. Have the children wind their toys and let them go.
3. Have each child individually dramatize being a wind-up toy. Have the rest of the children guess what the child is dramatizing. (Primarily for five year olds.)
4. At music time, sing the song "Johnny Works."

JOHNNY WORKS
Folk Song

John-ny works with one ham-mer, one ham-mer, one ham-mer,

John-ny works with one ham-mer, then he works with two,

1. One hammer—
   (Pound one fist)
2. Two hammers—
   (Pound two fists)
3. Three hammers—
   (Pound two fists and one foot)
4. Four hammers—
   (Pound two fists and two feet)
5. Five hammers—then he goes to sleep
   (Pound fist, feet and nod head)

5. During outside playtime, point out to the children that they are using their bodies to do work as they ride the tricycles, pump the swings, pull the wagons, etc.

B. ENERGY CAN BE CHANGED INTO ELECTRICAL ENERGY

Energy may be generated by several methods. Hydroelectric plants are places where flowing water is used to make electricity. The flowing water at a hydroelectric plant is held back by a large dam. This water has great force. As it is released, the flowing water turns wheels at the bottom of the dam. These wheels are parts of turbines which are connected to large generators. These generators produce electricity from the force of the water.

People change other forms of energy into electrical energy because electricity is easy to control and to move from one location to another. Most electricity is generated in electric power plants where coal, oil, or natural gas is burned to create steam which turns turbines and makes electricity. Wind can also be used to generate electricity.

1. Take a field trip with the children to a power-generating station. Back in the classroom, have the children describe the trip. As they do so, print their descriptions on a large sheet of newsprint or chart paper. When each child has made his or her contribution, read the children's "story" of their experience back to them. Post the "story" on a wall or bulletin board.
2. Using an electric skillet, make scrambled eggs with the children. Serve them at snack time.
3. Have an activity that uses the record player or filmstrip projector. Ask the children, "What kind of energy is the record player using?"

C. ENERGY MAKES MACHINES MOVE

People use machines to help them do work and move things from one location to another. The energy to make machines work comes from different sources. People use their own body energy to make some machines work. Some machines use the wind or electricity as their source of energy. Most vehicles use the fossil fuel oil as their source of energy. Oil and gasoline are stored in the vehicle and burned slowly to supply the vehicle with energy.

1. WE USE MACHINES TO GO FROM ONE PLACE TO ANOTHER

   a. At a group time, have the children list all of the gasoline-run machines they can think of that are used for transportation. Print the list on paper and tape it to the wall or put it on the bulletin board.
   b. Take the children on a field trip to a gas station. Watch the attendant service a car.
   c. Make a toy gas pump using a cardboard box. Have a service station dramatic play activity on the playground using tricycles for cars.

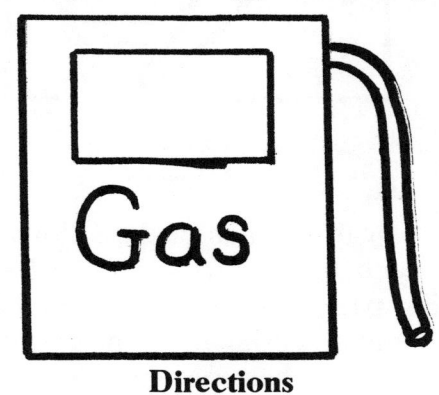

Directions

Use a large cardboard packing box to make a gas pump similar to the one above. Make a hole in the side of the box and insert a piece of rubber hose to be used for pumping the gas. Additional props such as tricycles for cars, a cash register and play money, attendants' hats, wash cloths, and an air pump may be used to enhance the dramatic play.

d. Visit a large construction site with the children. Observe the large machinery in use. Discuss the fuel used.

e. Make a machine or transportation collage using magazine pictures.

f. At music time, have the children move like cars, trains, boats, and other vehicles using the transportation record from the Peabody Language Development Kit (Level P) or other appropriate records.

g. Make a transportation lotto game. Play it with a group of children or let individual children use it as a matching game.

Directions

Make four charts by using each of the following pages as different chart patterns. Copy each page onto a standard size sheet of construction paper or drawing paper. Make single matching picture cards of each picture on the four charts using the same patterns. Mount each chart on a piece of cardboard. The picture cards and charts may be covered with clear contact paper for protection. Up to four children may participate in the game at one time. Give each child participating a chart. Hold up one picture card at a time and ask the children to identify it. Then ask who has the same picture on his chart. That child may then place the picture card on top of the matching picture on his chart. Continue until all of the picture cards have been used. Individual children may also use this as a matching game.

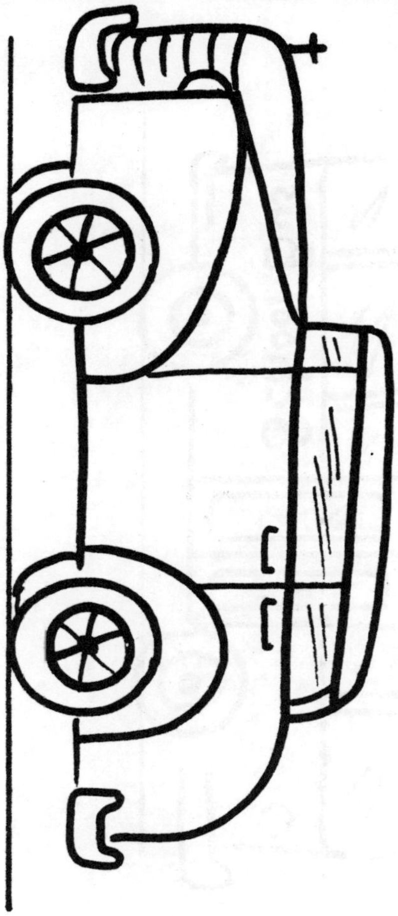

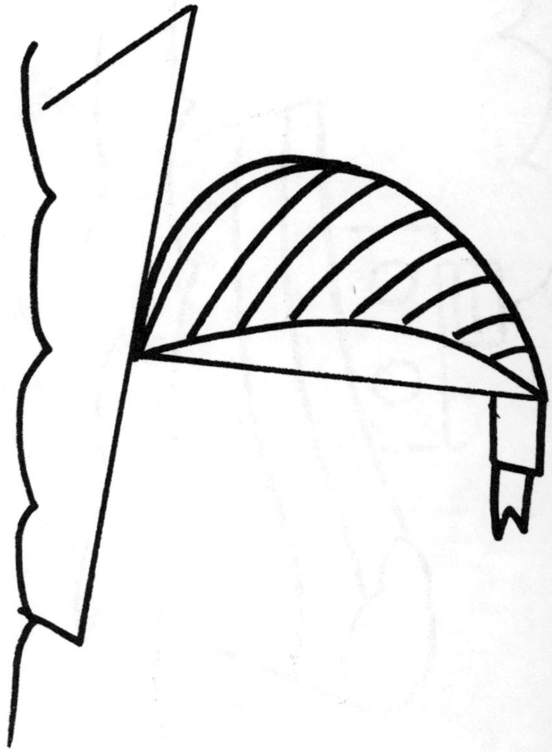

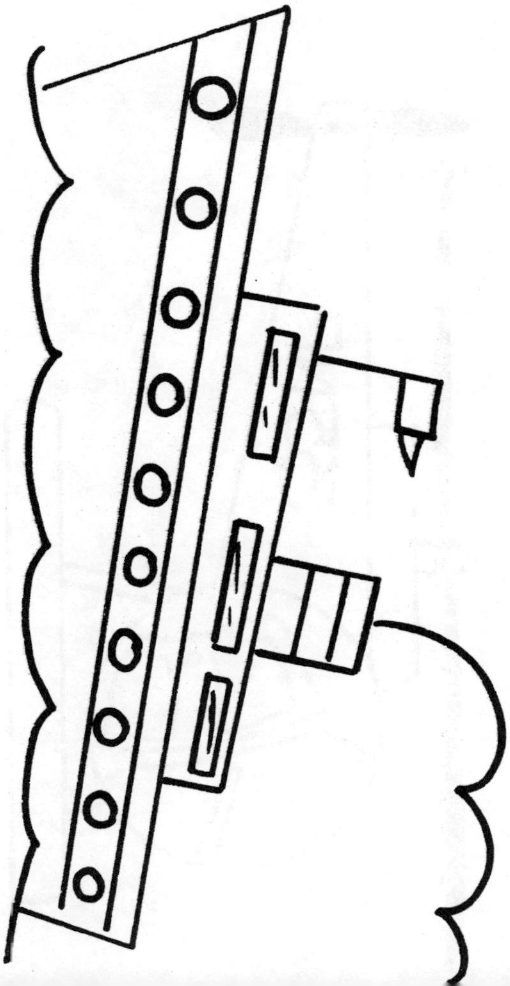

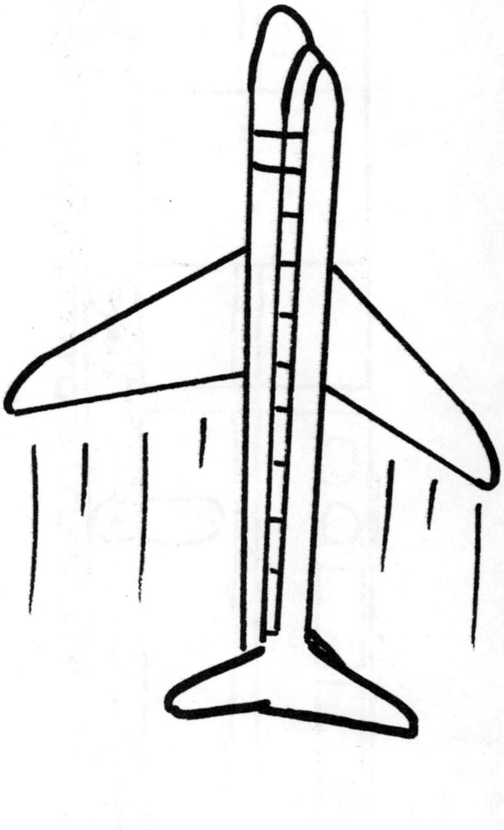

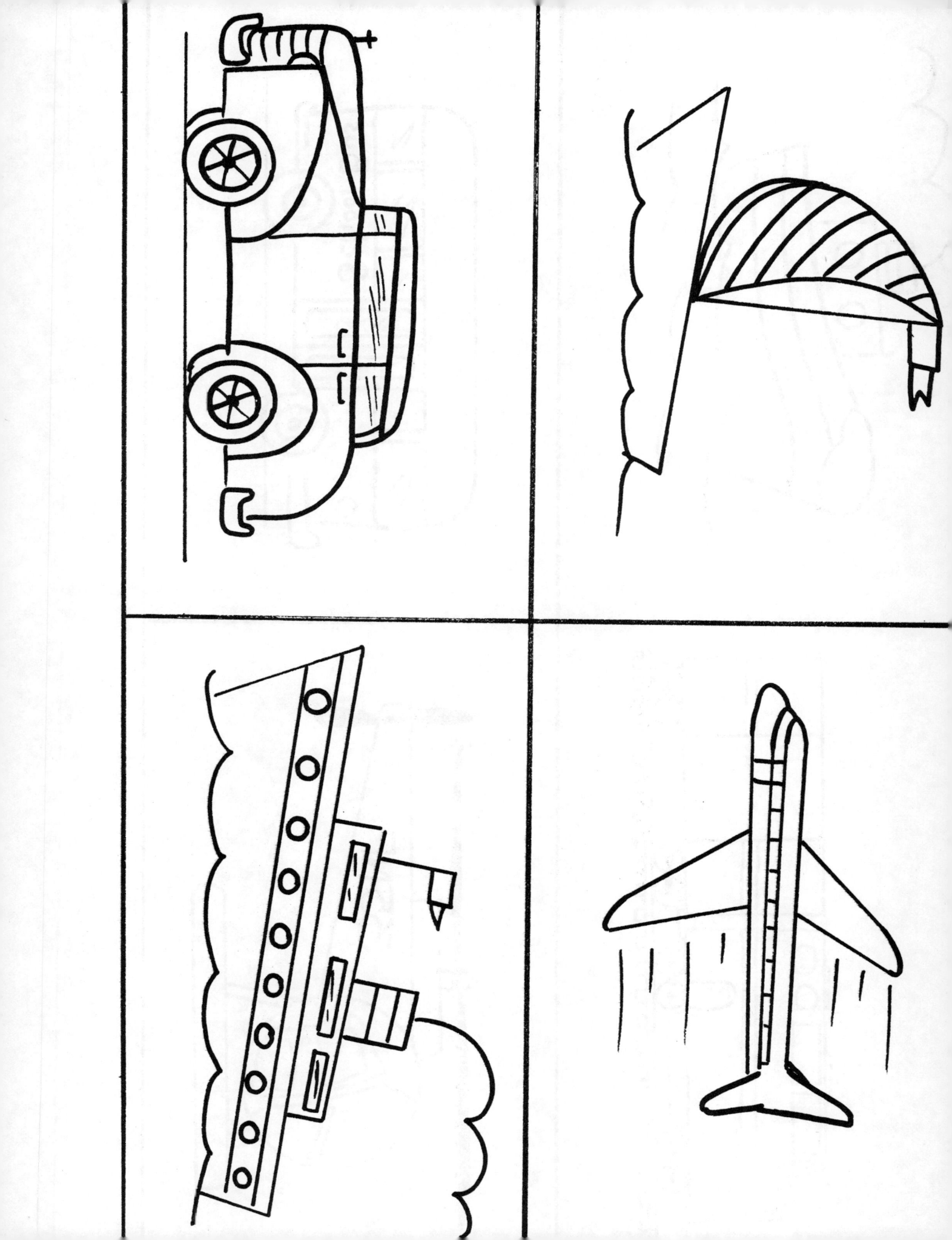

School Bus

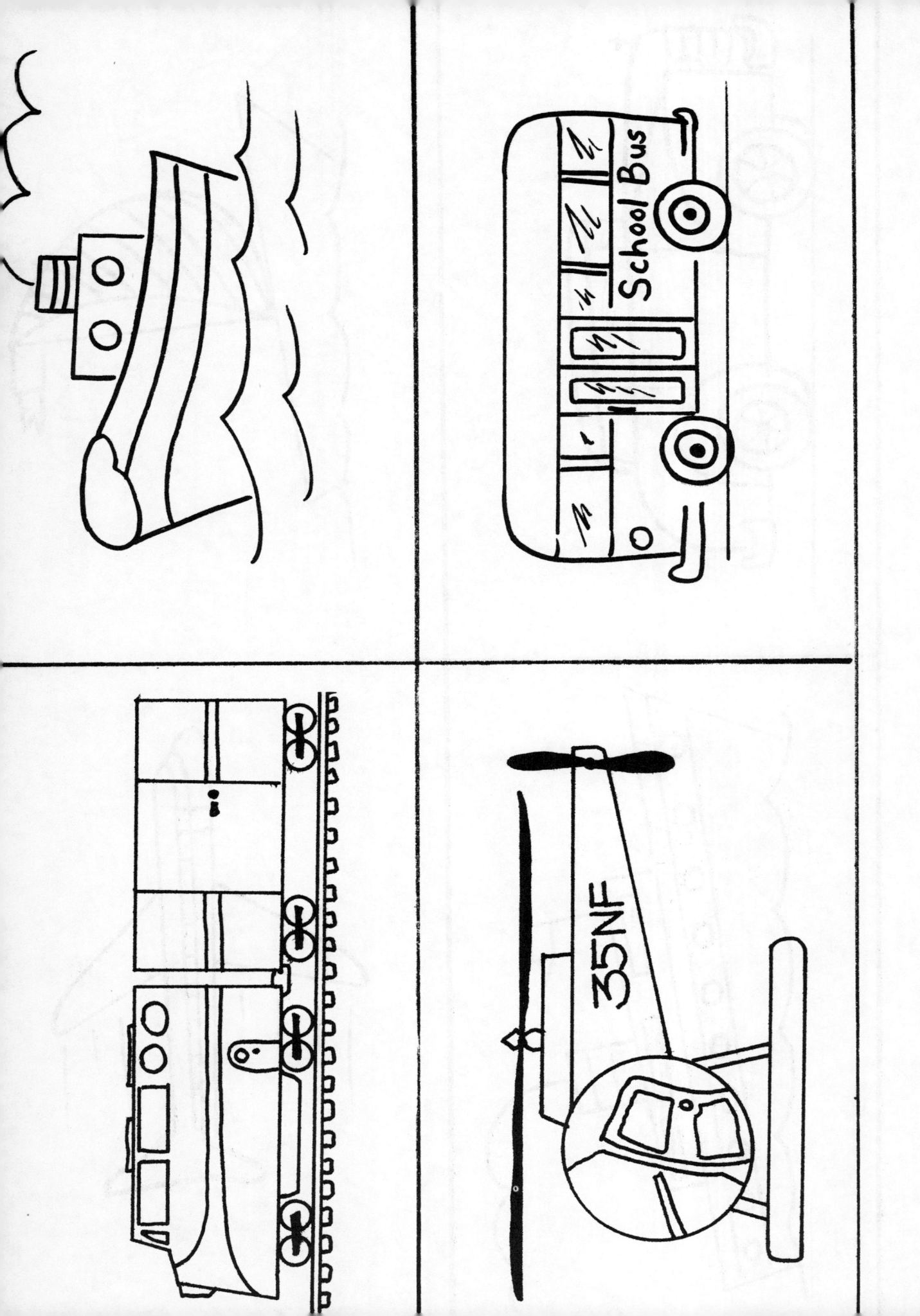

35NF

3261

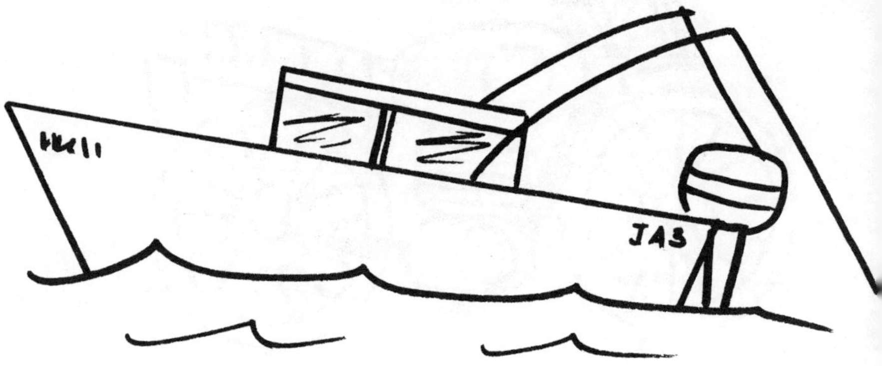

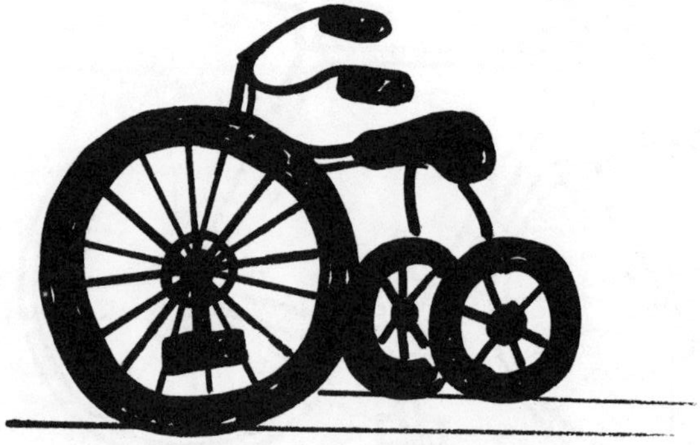

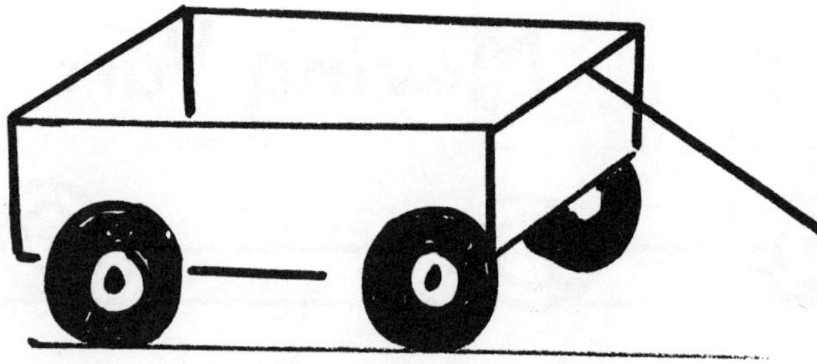

A & D

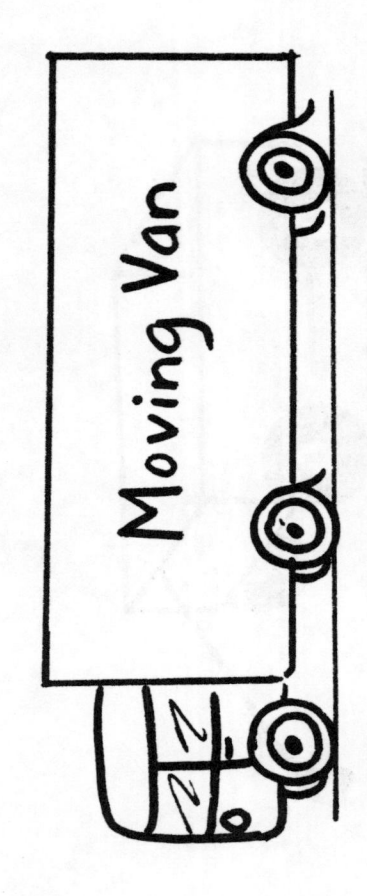

Moving Van

h. In the unit block area, provide props for airport or train play. Make a miniature fuel pump using a cardboard box. Encourage the children to fuel the vehicles.

i. Read *The Little Auto* to the children.

j. Read *Davy Goes Places* to the children.

2. WE USE MACHINES TO MAKE WORK EASIER

   a. Prepare two batches of whipped cream with the children. Have the children make one batch with a hand mixer and one batch with the electric mixer. Compare the ease with which they are made and the time it takes to whip it. Serve it on fruit at snack time.

b. On the playground, attach a block and tackle to a piece of high sturdy equipment. Attach a tricycle to the block and tackle. Have another tricycle of the same type on the ground nearby. Have the children, one at a time, lift the tricycle high off the ground using the block and tackle. Then ask them to lift the other tricycle with their hands. Compare the ease with which these two tasks are accomplished. Compare this experience to a steam shovel or tractor moving a heavy load. Teaching pictures from *Science for Beginners—Pictures That Teach* may be used to illustrate a later discussion of the experience.

- c. At group time, place a light but very bulky load such as four bed pillows on the floor. Ask a child to pick up the entire load at one time and transfer it across the room. The load will be so bulky the child will be unable to do so. Now bring in a cart or wagon and transfer the load to the cart or wagon. Ask: "Is the load easy to move now? Why?" Compare this to transporting loads by motor vehicle.
- d. Prepare two batches of ice cream with the children. Have the children make one batch in an electric ice cream freezer and the other batch in a hand-cranked freezer. Compare the ease with which the two batches are made and the time it takes to make them. Serve the ice cream at snack time.
- e. Read the book *Mike Mulligan and His Steam Shovel* to the children.

D. WE USE ENERGY IN OUR HOMES

People use energy in the homes for lighting, heating, cooling, food storage, food preparation, and recreation. Much of the energy that people use is in the form of electrical energy. Wires are used to bring electricity into buildings. These wires are conductors for electrons which are particles of electricity. The electrons move through the wires. This movement is called current electricity. Electrical wires inside homes and other buildings are run to places where lights, air conditioners, refrigerators and other appliances will be plugged in.

Fossil fuels are used in buildings for heat. These fuels are supplied to the building through pipes underground or stored at the building in a tank or pile. When needed they are burned slowly in a furnace to provide heat.

1. ENERGY IS USED TO LIGHT OUR HOMES

- a. Take a walk with the children. Point out street lights and electrical power lines running to buildings. Point out the power lines running to the school and their point of entry into the building.

b. Show the children the breaker box or fuse box in the school. Pull a breaker or fuse for the room you are in. When the lights go out, ask what has happened. Replace the breaker or fuse and repeat. Discuss the concept that electricity travels through the electrical wires. Use the pictures from *The Storm Book* to illustrate this concept.

c. Turn the lights in the classroom off during story time. After the story, discuss what life would be like if we didn't have electricity.

2. ENERGY IS USED TO HEAT WATER

a. Have the children's parents show the children where the water heater in their home is located. Have each child find out what fuel the water heater in his house uses. Make a list and tape it to the wall or put it on the bulletin board.

b. With the children, examine the water heater in the school. If it is a gas unit, look at the pilot light and the thermostat. If it is an electrical unit, look at the wires going into the heater and the thermostat. Discuss how a water heater works.

c. Take a one pound coffee can and paint it with black spray paint. Fill it with water. Have the children measure the temperature of the water with the thermometer and record it. Cap the can with a plastic lid and place it in the sun. Leave it for several days. Remove the lid and have the children measure the temperature of the water again and compare the temperatures. Discuss how larger solar water heaters work.

d. During group time, heat water on an electric hot plate. Observe how quickly the water boils. Make peppermint tea with the water and serve it at snack time.

3. ENERGY IS USED TO HEAT AND COOL OUR HOMES

a. With the children, examine the furnace in the school. If it is a gas unit, look at the pilot light and the thermostat. If it is an electrical unit, look at the wires going into the heater and the thermostat. Discuss how a furnace works.

b. Have the children's parents show the children where the furnace in their home is located. Have the children find out what fuel their home furnace uses. Make a list and post it on the wall or bulletin board.

c. Have the children make a collage using magazine pictures of furnaces and water heaters.

4. ENERGY IS USED TO COOK AND COOL FOOD

a. With a group of children watching, pull the fuse that supplies electricity to the school kitchen. Open the refrigerator door. Note that the light is out. If possible, leave the electricity off for several hours. Place a thermometer in the open refrigerator. Measure the temperature at half-hour intervals and record each time. Discuss what happens and why.

b. Unplug the refrigerator and defrost it with the children.

c. If the school stove is electric, pull the fuse or plug with the children watching. Turn the oven on. Observe that it does not get hot.

d. If the school stove is gas, take the top off with the children watching. Show them the pilot light and the tubes to the burners. With the children standing well away, turn on a burner. Discuss with them how the stove works.

e. Make jello with the children using an electric hot plate to boil the water. Separate the liquid jello into two pans. Cool one pan in the refrigerator and the other pan on the counter. Discuss what happens. Serve it for a snack.

f. Have the children fill two ice cube trays with water. Put one tray in the freezer. Put the other tray on the counter. Leave them overnight. Discuss what happens.

5. ENERGY IS USED TO HAVE FUN

a. Have the children make a list of all the electrical appliances in their homes that are used for recreational purposes, such as radio, television, stereo, toys, etc. Have pictures of these items to show as you discuss them.

b. Have the children bring their favorite energy-user or a picture of it to school for "show and tell."

c. Have the children paint a mural to music. Comment on the energy being used by the record player or radio.

d. In a small group, pop popcorn on an electric hot plate. Count out enough paper cups for each child and staff person. Fill the cups with popcorn. Set up a movie theater using the electric filmstrip projector and electric record player. Give the children play money and let them buy admission to the All-Electric Movie Theater during free play. During intermission let them buy popcorn.

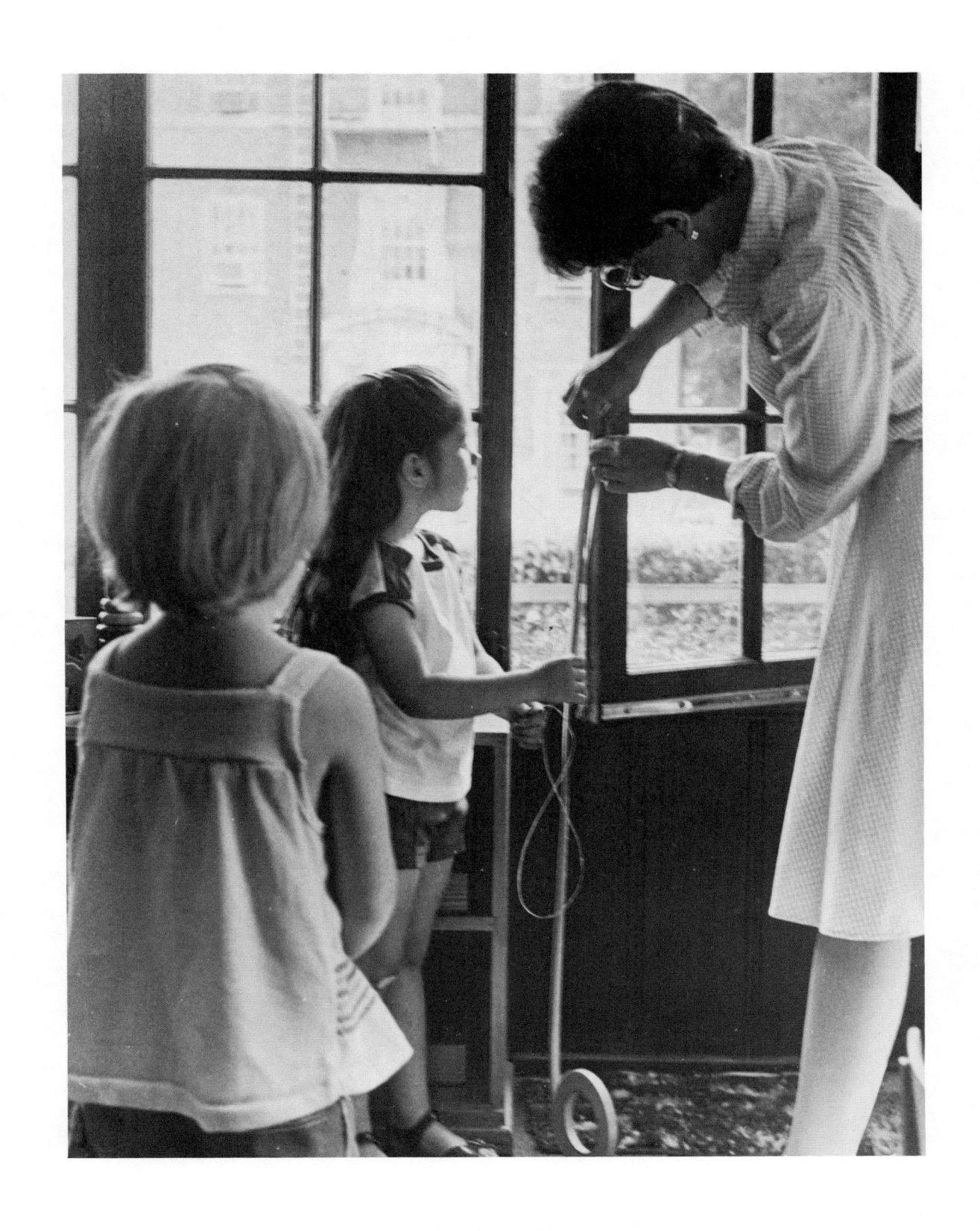

IV. WISE ENERGY USE

A. WE NEED TO SAVE ENERGY

People have been successful on earth largely because of their ability to control energy. The earth has two types of energy resources. Renewable resources are those which can be used many times or can be replaced, such as wind, flowing water and the sun. Nonrenewable resources are those which can be used only once and cannot be replaced, such as coal, oil and natural gas.

Saving energy through wise energy use is called conservation. Conservation helps people control the rate at which nonrenewable energy resources are consumed.

1. SAVING ENERGY IS CALLED CONSERVATION

   a. Read selected parts of the book *My Energy Ant Book* to the children. Some of the material will be beyond the children's comprehension and should be omitted or adapted to their level of understanding.

2. CONSERVATION OF ENERGY SAVES MONEY

   a. Take the children on a car trip to the gas station. Put gas in the car. Have the children pay for the gas.

   Provide props for a gas station dramatic play activity (gas pump and hose, tricycles, cash register, rags, hats, air pump, and oil cans). Give the participating children play money to pay for the gas they buy.

c. Show the children the electric meter at the school. Turn off all of the electrical appliances in the school. See that the meter stops. Turn an appliance on. Watch the dials move. Discuss the fact that the meter records how much electricity we use and that the electric company charges us for the amount we use.

d. Have the children find out where the electric meter is at their home.

B. THERE ARE MANY WAYS TO USE ENERGY WISELY

Wise energy use requires that people change their attitudes and lifestyles to reflect a desire to save nonrenewable energy resources. Conservation is successful when everyone cooperates to make it work. There are many ways to conserve energy. Some easy ways to conserve energy are: turning off unneeded lights, walking more and driving fewer miles, and keeping the thermostat down in the winter and up in the summer.

1. WE CAN USE ENERGY WISELY BY USING LESS ELECTRICITY AND FOSSIL FUEL

a. Have the children share in the responsibility of turning off the classroom lights when going outside to play. Discuss how turning off the lights saves energy.

b. On a cold day, open a window or door in the same room where the school thermostat is located. Have the children watch the temperature reading on the thermostat or on a thermometer. Note that as the room cools, the heat comes on. Discuss the importance of keeping windows and doors closed in cold weather.

c. Have the children test an outside door of the school by sliding a quarter under the door. If it slides through easily, the door needs weatherstripping. Weatherstrip it with the children.

d. Have each child bring a sweater to school to keep in his locker. Show the children the furnace thermostat. Discuss lowering the temperature two degrees to save energy. Explain that a sweater insulates the body and equals two degrees of added warmth. Lower the thermostat and put on the sweaters. (Primarily for four and five year olds.)

e. Hold a candle in front of a drafty window. Have the children observe the flame blowing. Weatherstrip the window with the children. Repeat the experiment. Discuss heat loss.

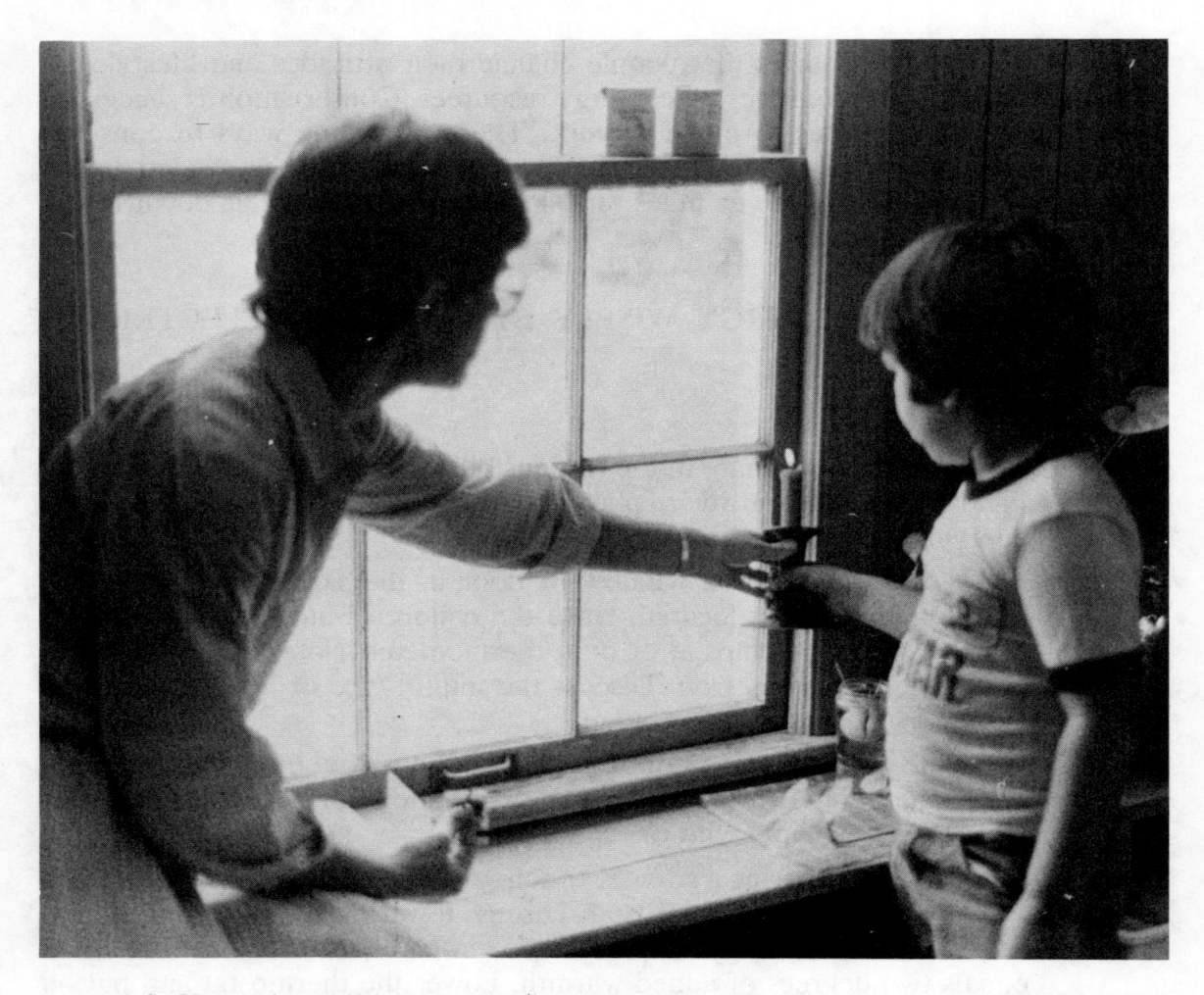

f. Have the children wash the dishes after their snack instead of using the dishwasher. Discuss the energy saved.

g. Make a list with the children of all the ways they can think of to use energy wisely. Mimeograph the list and send one copy home with each child.

h. In a small group or at group time, show pictures of energy being used wisely and energy not being used wisely. Discuss with the group what in the picture tells them it is wise or unwise use of energy. Have them give examples of how they can use energy wisely in their own homes.

(a)

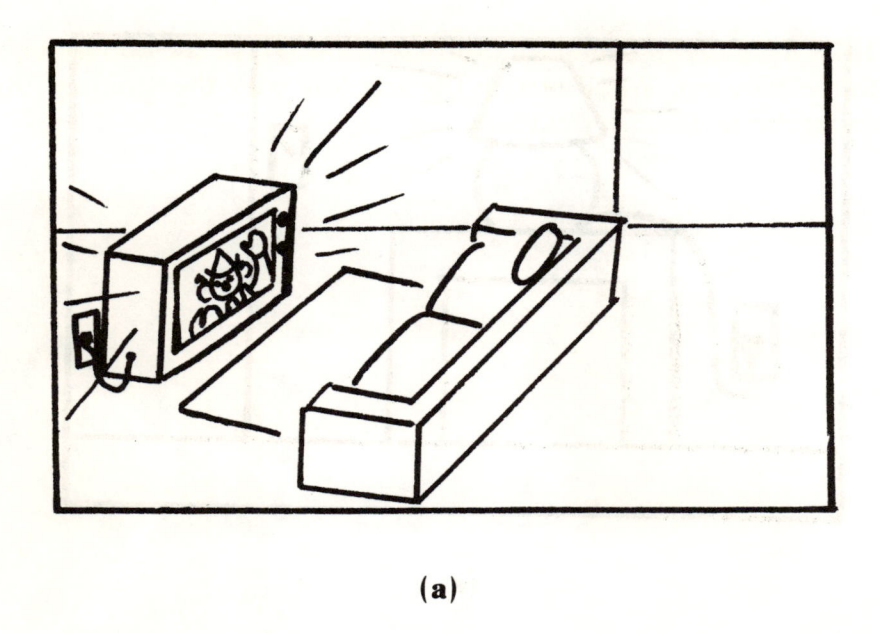

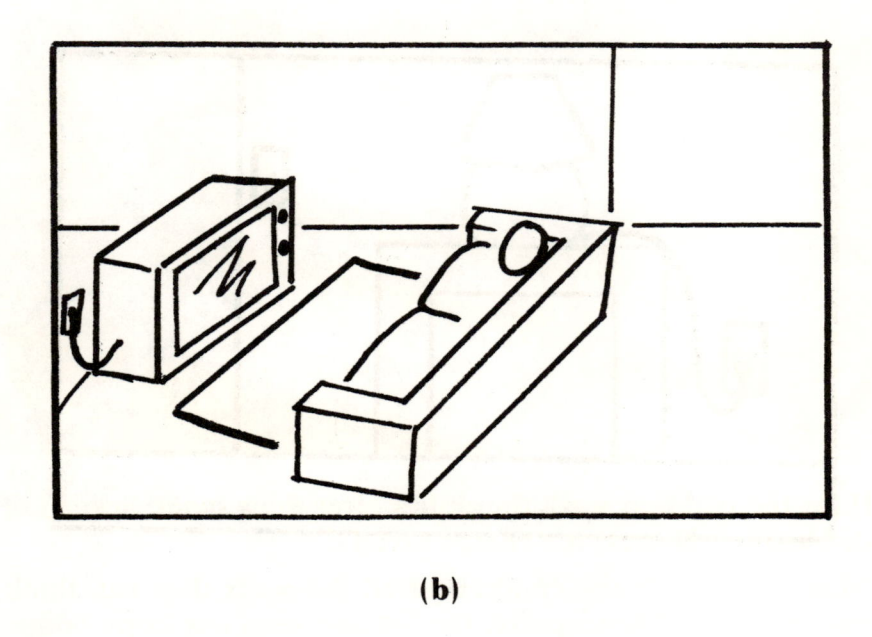

(b)

Directions

Draw pictures similar to these on a larger scale using a standard size sheet of construction paper or drawing paper for each picture. Using picture (a), ask the children questions such as "What's happening in this picture?" "Is anyone in the room?" "Does the T.V. need to be on if no one is in the room?" "Why?" Using picture (b), ask the children "Is energy being used wisely in this picture?" "Why?"

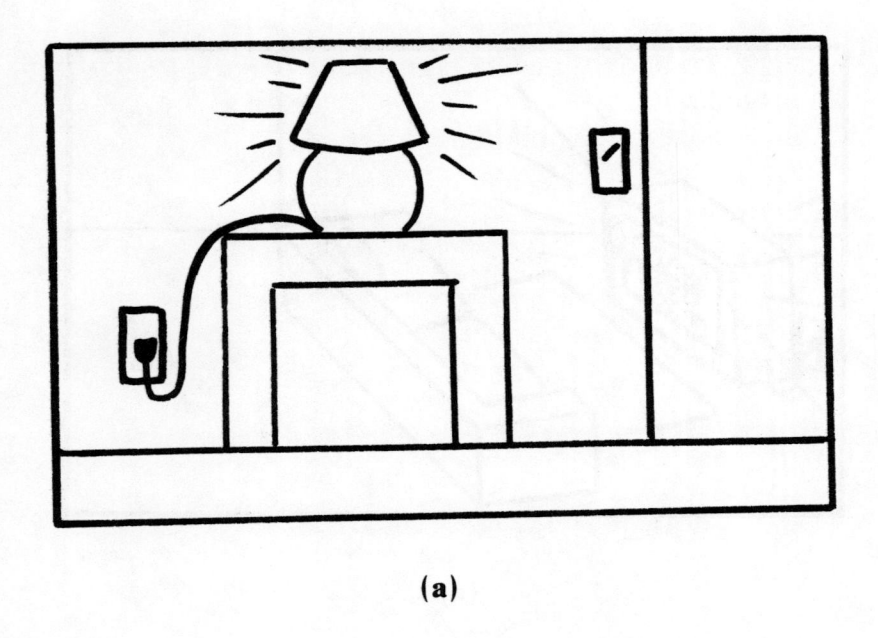

(a)

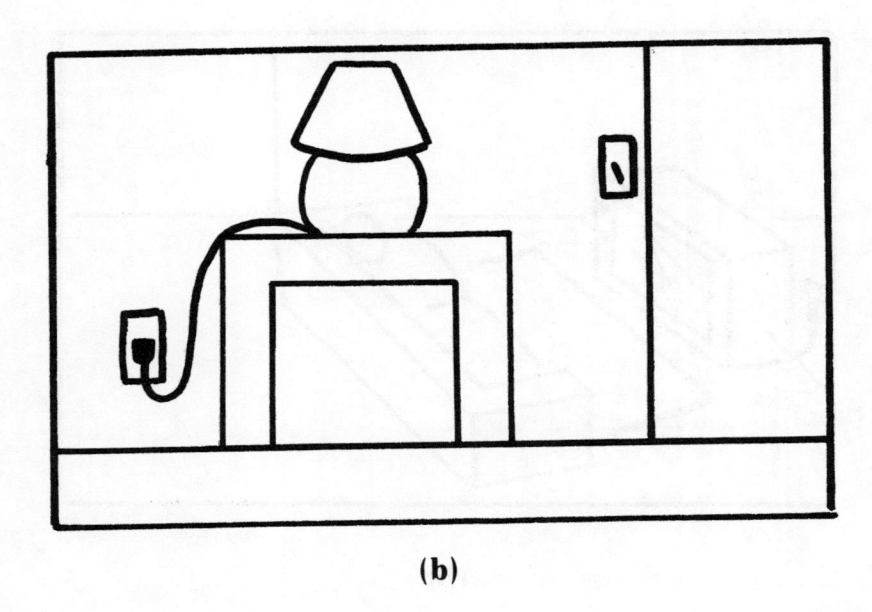

(b)

Directions

Draw pictures similar to these on a larger scale using a standard size sheet of construction paper or drawing paper for each picture. Using picture (a), ask the children questions such as "What's happening in this picture?" "Is anyone in the room?" "Does the light need to be on if no one is in the room?" "Why?" Using picture (b), ask the children "Is energy being used wisely in this picture?" "Why?"

i. As a summary activity, select parts of the Federal Energy Administrative slide presentations, *What Is Energy?* and *What Is Energy Conservation?* and show them to the children.

APPENDIX A

BACKGROUND READING FOR TEACHERS

Coughlin, S. "The Politics of Energy." *National Voter,* Summer 1977 (newsletter published by League of Women Voters).

National Geographic, February, 1981 (issue devoted to energy).

Energy Conservation Experiments You Can Do. Southfield, Michigan: Thomas Alva Edison Foundation, 1974.

"Energy and the Schools." *Today's Education,* September-October, 1977, pp. 54-64.

Our Energy Problems and Solutions. Malvern, Pennsylvania: Energy Conservation Research, 1977.

Tips For Energy Savers. Federal Energy Administration FEA/D 77/212, August, 1977.

Journal of Home Economics, Winter, 1978 (issue devoted to energy conservation).

APPENDIX B

SELECTED REFERENCES FOR USE WITH THE ENERGY CURRICULUM

BOOKS

Barnett, J. *The Wind Thief.* New York: Atheneum, 1977.

Brown, M. *The Steamroller.* New York: Walker and Company, 1974.

Burton, V. L. *Mike Mulligan and the Steam Shovel.* Boston: Houghton Mifflin, 1939.

Cartwright, S. *Sunlight.* New York: Corvane, McCann and Gerhegar, Inc., 1974.

Gondey, A. *The Day We Saw the Sun Come Up.* New York: Scribner, 1976.

Green, M., and McBurney, M. *Is It Hard? Is It Easy?* New York: Young Scott Books, 1960.

Hall, M. *Gilberto and The Wind.* New York: Viking, 1963.

Hoban, T. *Dig Drill—Dump Fill.* New York: Greenwillow Books, 1975.

Hurd, E. *The Day the Sun Danced.* New York: Harper and Row, 1965.

Janosch, C. *The Yellow Auto Named Ferdinand.* Minneapolis: Rhoda Books, 1973.

Kaufman, J. *The Boat Book.* New York: Golden Press, 1965.

Lenski, L. *The Little Auto.* New York: Henry Z. Walck, 1934.

Lenski, L. *Davy Goes Places.* New York: Henry Z. Walck, 1962.

Lionni, L. *Alexander and the Wind-Up Mouse.* New York: Pantheon, 1969.

Maestro, B. *In My Boat.* New York: Thomas Y. Crowell, 1976.

McGovern, A. *Stone Soup.* New York: Scholastic Book Services, 1968.

Meeks, E. *One is the Engine.* Chicago: Follett, 1956.

Polendorf, I. *The True Book of Energy.* Chicago: Children's Press, 1963.

Rey, H. A. *Curious George Rides a Bike.* Boston: Houghton Mifflin, 1952.

Scott, W. R. *The Water That Jack Drank.* New York: William R. Scott, 1950.

Swift, H. *The Little Red Lighthouse and the Great Gray Bridge.* New York: Harcourt, Brace and World, 1942.

Tresselt, A. *Follow the Wind.* New York: Lothrop, Lee and Shepard, Inc., 1950.

Zolotow, C. *The Storm Book.* New York: Harper and Brothers, 1952.

My Energy Ant Book. Washington, D.C.: Federal Energy Administration, 1976.

SONGS

Jaye, M.T. *Making Music Your Own K.* Atlanta: Silver Burdett, 1966.

Landeck, B. *More Songs to Grow On.* New York: William Sloane Associates, Inc., 1954.

Smith, R. and Leonhard, C. *Discovering Music Together: Early Childhood.* Chicago: Follett Publishing Company, 1968.

The Kindergarten Book. Boston: Ginn and Company, 1959.

Sesame Street Songbook, Vol. I. New York: Quadrangle, The New York Times Book Company, 1972.

Singing Fun. Atlanta: Webster Publishing Company, 1954.

RECORDS

Movin'. Hap Palmer, AR 546, Educational Activities, Inc., Freeport, New York

Nothing To Do. Children's Record Guild, 1-12-A, New York, New York.

Physical Fitness for Preschool Children. LaCrone, RRC-703, Rhythm Record Company, Oklahoma City, Oklahoma.

Sounds Around Us—Sounds of Ways to Travel. American Guidance Services, Circle Pines, Minnesota.

OTHER RESOURCES

Energy Ant Slide/Tape Presentation, "What Is Energy?" "What Is Energy Conservation?" Available from Federal Energy Administration, Office of Communication and Public Affairs, Washington, D.C., or from your local power company.

Little Ideas. An early childhood nutrition program, produced and distributed by the National Dairy Council, 1973.

Peabody Language Development Kit (Level P)

Science for Beginners—Pictures That Teach. Morristown, New Jersey: Silver Burdett, 1965.

APPENDIX C

Energy Knowledge of Preschool Children Following an Energy Education Program

The purpose of this study was to determine what knowledge of energy concepts three, four, and five year old children possessed and if their knowledge increased as a result of an energy education program. The participants were the children enrolled in The University of Alabama Child Development Laboratory. The data for this study were obtained during the spring semester, 1980.

The sample was composed of forty-seven children: fifteen three year old children, eighteen four year old children and fourteen five year old children. Twenty-one of the participants were males and twenty-six were females. The children were primarily from middle class homes and represented a variety of nationalities and cultures.

The instrument used in this study, the Preschool Test of Energy Information, was developed by the investigators. The teachers of the children developed the concepts in the areas of: what energy is, sources of energy, uses of energy and wise energy use. They did not participate in or contribute to the development of the test. The test was composed of forty-two items. The test was designed to be administered individually and consisted of a series of pictures and objects arranged in groups of four. The children were asked to identify one item in each group by pointing to it or picking it up.

The following null hypotheses were tested and subjected to analysis of variance to determine the interaction of age and sex and the difference in pre- and post-test scores.

1. There are no significant differences in the amount of knowledge the group of preschool children have relating to energy before and after the presentation of an energy education program.
2. There are no significant differences between younger and older children in the amount of gain between pre-test and post-test scores of energy knowledge following the completion of the energy education program.
3. There are no significant differences between boys and girls in the amount of knowledge relating to energy before and after the energy education program.

Following the pretest, the teachers of the children in the Child Development Laboratory conducted a three week energy education program. Immediately following the energy education program the Preschool Test of Energy Information was again administered to the children.

The results of the study revealed that:

1. There was a significant difference in the amount of knowledge the groups of preschool children had relating to energy before and after the energy education program was presented.
2. All age groups and both sexes profited from the energy education project. There was no significant interaction between age, sex and change in pretest and post-test scores. Interestingly, the three year old group as a whole made greater gains than did the four and five year old groups even though this difference was not statistically significant.
3. There were no significant differences between boys and girls in the amount of knowledge relating to energy before and after the energy education program.

It would have been interesting to determine how much information the children retained over a period of time but this was not a part of the study. In addition, it would have been desirable to determine how much of the knowledge carried over into the home. Future research could explore these questions.

WE'LL HELP YOU TO HELP THEM.

EDUCATION

108-80 LOOKING AT CHILDREN. Richard Goldman, Ph.D.; Johanne Peck, Ph.D.; Stephen Lehane, Ed.D. Combines theory and practice, exploring such issues as language development, classification, play and moral development in children. Also includes a look at sex typing, television, single-parent families, and the fathers role in parenting. $12.95

407-80 ALTERNATIVE APPROACHES TO EDUCATING YOUNG CHILDREN. Martha Abbott, Ph.D.; Brenda Galina, Ph.D.; Robert Granger, Ph.D., Barry Klein, Ph.D. Delves into the theoretical basis behind three major programmatic approaches to education: programs emphasizing skill development; cognitive growth; and affective development. This book encourages the reader to develop his or her own theoretical and philosophical position. Each approach is discussed according to rationale and Philosophy, Curriculum Goals, Planning of Instruction, Use of Physical Space, Instructional Materials, Evaluation Methods, and the Instructional Role of the Teacher and Child. $6.95

413-80 YOUNG CHILDREN'S BEHAVIOR. Johanne Peck, Ph.D. Approaches to discipline and guidance to help the readers deal more effectively with young children. Six units focus on "Examining Your Goals," "Looking At Behavior," "Young Children's Views of Right, Wrong and Rules," "Applying Behavior Modification," and "Supporting Childs Needs." $7.95

406-80 THE WHOLE TEACHER. Kathy R. Thornburg, Ph.D. Designed for education majors and teachers of early childhood programs, this book presents a unified approach to teacher training. Topics addressed include: personal attitues, curriculum planning and development; classroom management techniques; working with volunteers, staff and parents; and professional development. $12.95

418-80 ORIENTATION TO PRE-SCHOOL ASSESSMENT. T. Thomas McMurrain. Designed for the child development center staff, this handbook presents a clear description of the effective assessment of the individual child. In addition, this manual is the user's guide to HUMANICS CHILD DEVELOPMENT ASSESSMENT FORM, a developmental checklist of skills and behavior that normally emerge during the 3 to 6 year range. Includes 5 assessment tools. $14.95

419A-80 COMPETENCIES: A SELF STUDY GUIDE FOR TEACHING COMPETENCIES IN EARLY CHILDHOOD. Mary E. Kasindorf. Divided into six competency areas and thirteen functional areas of competence as identified by the Child Development Consortium. This guide can be used to identify existing teaching skills and training needs. Designed to serve as an aid for those preparing for the C.D.A. credital. It contains checklists of teacher and child behaviors and activities that would indicate competence and can be used in assembling a C.D.A. portfolio. $12.95

humanics
Post Office Box 7447
Atlanta, Georgia 30309

PROJECT IDEAS

416-80 AEROSPACE PROJECTS FOR YOUNG CHILDREN. Jane Caballero, Ph.D. This "first of it's kind" manual provides teachers and young students with an overview of aerospace history from kites and balloons, on to helicopters, gliders and airplanes, through todays satellites and the space shuttle. Each chapter is followed by interdisciplinary activities and field trip suggestions. $12.95

403-80 MATH MAGIC. Filled with ideas for creating a stimulating pre-school learning environment, this book encourages active participation in the learning process. Through songs, limericks, puzzles, games, and personal involvement it will help children become accustomed to basic math principles, such as classification, seriation, the development of logical thinking, as well as teaching them basic problem solving skills. Comes with "Magic Pouch" which contains full size games, puzzles, bulletin board aids and whimsical animals (17 x 24) as a supplement to the text. $12.95

Vol. I, 409-80, Vol. II, 410-80. WHEN I GROW UP. Michele Kavanaugh, Ph.D. Provides activities for expanding the human potential of male and female students, while eliminating sex-role stereotypes. Volume I contains experiences for pre-kindergarten thru 8th grade students. Volume II continues with input suitable for high school through young adulthood.
$10.95 ea.

408-80 METRIC MAGIC. Kathy R. Thornburg, Ph.D. and James L. Thornburg, Ph.D. A fun book of creative classroom activities, *Metric Magic* was developed to teach preschoolers through sixth graders to think "metric." Includes action oriented activities involving the concept of length and progress through mass, area, volume, capacity, time, speed, and temperature. $8.95

417-80 ART PROJECTS FOR YOUNG CHILDREN. Jane Caballero, Ph.D. Over 100 stimulating projects for pre-school and elementary age children, including: drawing; painting; cut and paste; flannel and bulletin boards; puppets; clay; printing; textiles; and photography. Designed for those with limited budget and time schedule. Success oriented. $12.95

400-A CHILD'S PLAY. Barbara Trencher, M.S. A fun-filled activities and material book which goes from puppets and mobiles to poetry and songs, to creatively fill the pre-schoolers day. This handbook is a natural addition to a CDA or other competency-based learning program and has been used nation-wide for this purpose. $12.95

415-80 DESIGNING EDUCATIONAL MATERIALS FOR YOUNG CHILDREN. Jane Cabellero, Ph.D. A competency based approach providing over 125 illustrated activities encompassing language arts, health and safety, puppetry, math, and communication skills. Suggested functional areas and stated purpose for each activity make this a valuable tool for the CDA candidate. $14.95

PARENT INVOLVEMENT

419-80 FAMILY ENRICHMENT TRAINING. Gary Wilson and T. Thomas McMurrain. Designed for a workshop of six sessions, this program focuses on concerns for families today including communication, family relations, discipline, and developing self-esteem. Techniques such as role playing, small and large group interaction, and journals encourage participants to develop greater understanding of themselves and others. This package includes a manual for trainers, a participants "log" and the booklet "Dialog for Parents." $12.95

102-80 PARENTS AND TEACHERS. Gary B. Wilson. Offers strategies for staff trainers or anyone involved in parent or adult education. Included are training techniques which facilitate group interaction, team building, effective communication and self awareness. Designed to build a program promoting increased parent-staff interaction, each activity includes clear instructions, stated objectives, lists of materials and time requirements. $12.95

106-80 WORKING TOGETHER. Anthony J. Colleta, Ph.D. This practical handbook includes: plans for parent participation in the classroom; alternative approaches to teaching parenting skills; ideas for home based activities; and supplements to parent programs in the form of child development guides and checklists. $12.95

107-80 WORKING PARENTS. Susan Brown and Pat Kornhauser. Designed to make a positive impact on the family life of working parents, this book presents techniques which promote constructive and enjoyable parent-child interaction without disrupting the families daily routine. $12.95

24 Hour Direct Mail Service: 404-874-2176

420-80 BUILDING SUCCESSFUL PARENT-TEACHER PARTNERSHIPS. Kevin J. Swick, Ph.D., Carol F. Hobson, Ph.D. and R. Eleanor Duff, Ph.D. Deals with the issues of parent involvement by including: an in depth examination of the changing nature of parenting and teaching in recent decades — the emergence of the two-parent working family, the vanishing extended family, the one-parent working family, and a comprehensive plan for implementing successful parent-teacher programs. $10.00

ASSESSMENT

CD-507 CABS — CHILDREN ADAPTIVE SCALE. Bert O. Richmond and Richard H. Kicklighter. A testing tool for children ages 5-10 years. Created to measure skills in the following areas: (1) language development; (2) independent functioning; (3) family role performance; (4) economic-vocational activity and (5) socialization. Useful for enabling teachers to plan remediation for the child's level of adaptive behavior. Designed to be administered directly to the child.
Manual $19.95   Student Test Booklet $.65 ea.

ADOLESCENTS

411A-80 I LIVE HERE, TOO. Wanda Grey. Designed for the teacher who would like to improve the atmosphere in the classroom by helping each student to develop a more positive self concept. Themes such as "You Are One Of A Kind," "Know How You Feel," "You And Other People," "As Others See You," and "Using Your Creativity," will foster in children a better understanding of themselves and the people around them. $8.95

414S-80 H.E.L.P. FOR THE ADOLESCENT. Norma Banas, M.Ed. and J. H. Wills, M.S. Explores the underlying causes of the problems of the high school underachiever or potential dropout. Useful tests, programs and reading references are included to help identify "learning weaknesses" and promote "learning strengths." $6.95

humanics
Post Office Box 7447
Atlanta, Georgia 30309

SOCIAL SERVICES

302-80 ASSESSING STAFF DEVELOPMENT NEEDS. Gary B. Wilson, Gerald Pavloff and Larry Linkes. Provides a step-by-step methodology for determining the training needs of child development programs and planning their resolution. Tear-out worksheets and staff questionnaires will help clarify job descriptions and goal definitions, in conjunction with the needs assessment. $3.00

206-80 A SYSTEM FOR RECORD KEEPING. Gary B. Wilson, T. Thomas McMurrain and Barbara Trencher. Designed for family oriented social service agencies. This handbook is an integral part of HUMANICS Record Keeping System and should be used as a guide to proper use of the HUMANICS Record Keeping Forms. $12.95

201-80 INTERVENTION IN HUMAN CRISIS. T. Thomas McMurrain, Ph.D. Clearly presented intervention strategies based on an evaluation of crisis intensity and the response capacity of the individual or family. Rights, risks and responsibilities of the helper are also discussed. $6.95

MAINSTREAMING

404S-80 NEW APPROACHES TO SUCCESS IN THE CLASSROOM. Norma Banas, M.Ed. and J. A. Wills, M.S. A companion volume to Identifying Early Learning Gaps, designed for mainstream children in kindergarten through third grade. Includes activities structured to inspire the student who has experienced repeated failure and to help him or her acquire learning skills in the areas of reading, writing and arithmetic. Can be used in the classroom for the entire group or for a small group. $12.95

412S-80 LATON: THE PARENT BOOK. Mary Tom Riley, Ed.D. Presents a training plan for parents of handicapped children, designed to acquaint them with the resources, facilities, educational opportunities and diagnostic processes available to help them raise their children. This easy to read book will encourage parents to get involved. $12.95

New Publications

REALTALK: EXERCISES IN FRIENDSHIP AND HELPING SKILLS. George M. Gazda, Ed.D., William C. Childers, Ph.D., Richard P. Walters, Ph. D. A human relations training program for secondary school students including student text and instructor manual. REALTALK includes training in getting along with others, making and keeping friends, leadership, helping others deal with their problems, and learning how to talk with practically anyone about practically anything.

THE LOLLYPOP TEST: A DIAGNOSTIC SCREENING TEST OF SCHOOL READINESS. Alex L. Chew, Ed.D. A lollypop loved by all. Children will enjoy taking this test for school readiness, educators will appreciate the easy quick, and significant results. Purpose of the test: (1) to assist the schools in identifying children needing additional readiness activities before entering first grade (2) to identify children with special problems and (3) to assist schools in planning individual and group instructional objectives. Culture-Free.

**SPECIAL INTRODUCTORY PRICE
$14.95 each**

ORDER FORM

ORDER NO.	TITLE/DESCRIPTION	QUANTITY	PRICE

Subtotal ....
Ga. residents add 4% sales tax .....
Add shipping and handling charges .....
TOTAL ....

Make checks payable to:
HUMANICS LIMITED
P. O. Box 7447
Atlanta, Georgia 30309

Ship to:

NAME _____
ORGANIZATION _____
ADDRESS _____
CITY _____ STATE _____ ZIP _____

(AREA CODE) TELEPHONE NO.

Institutional P.O. No. _____
Date _____

Shipping and Handling Charges

Up to $10.00 add	$1.25
$10.01 to $20.00 add	$2.25
$20.01 to $40.00 add	$3.25
$40.01 to $70.00 add	$4.25
$70.01 to $100.00 add	$5.25
$100.01 to $125.00 add	$6.25
$125.01 to $150.00 add	$7.25
$150.01 to $175.00 add	$8.25
$175.01 to $200.00 add	$9.25

Orders over $200. vary depending on method of shipment.